I0469191

The Four Elements of Thinking

Reasoning, Creativity, Synthesis, Evaluation

REFRESHER Version

By Benjamin Cheung, Ph.D.

ISBN: 978-1-0731-4378-8

Table of Contents

Tables

Preface

This refresher edition of the Four elements of thinking serves as a compact pocket companion to the full edition. This slimmed down version of the Four elements has removed all the examples, thought exercises, element summaries, and metaphor descriptions. This would make for a dry first read; but a functional refresher if you are already familiar with the Four elements of thinking. This refresher assumes you have read the original book and want to refresh your memory of the Four elements of thinking. I have gone through every sentence of the original edition of the book with the aim of slimming down the book while preserving as much of the essence of the original book as possible. So, the actual descriptions of each of the components were the least effected. The Elements component & principles summary appendices have been kept because they summarize the Four elements in the most compact form possible.

The four elements book was originally motivated by my goal to find an efficient system to improve thinking. People think every waking minute of every day. For such an important activity, we should strive to improve our ability. How often do you think about thinking? Some can quickly identify the main idea, the "big picture", the root cause, the underlying principles and focus in on the key issues. They are natural problem solvers. Some have a talent for thinking. With practice and training you can hone your innate aptitude even further.

The reason for a gap in thinking ability between individuals is that thinking is a skill. First, you must recognize that thinking is a skill that can be improved. Unfocused, your mind will aimlessly wander. A professional learns a trade over years of dedicated study and practice. An engineer, physicist, or mathematician can manipulate equations and handle numbers better than most individuals. These professionals seem to juggle complex concepts in their mind with the grace of a dancer. They reason logically and methodically break down a complex problem.

This book identifies four aspects of thinking: reasoning, creativity, synthesis, evaluation. These are essential to productive thinking. They form the basis of effective thinking skills. Techniques are presented which will allow you to methodically improve each of these four aspects of thinking.

This book is written to be timeless work. Higher thinking will persist through time. If higher thought exists, the need for structured thinking will exist. This was the motivation for the original book. Structured thinking is a skill, that can be honed and practiced like any other skill. As such, it requires practice and employing techniques to develop good thinking habits.

Exploring the key aspects of thinking was the primary motivation for writing this book. What is a subject that is timeless and will always be relevant? Thinking about thinking. What are the principle aspects of thinking? The answer to that question starts the quest which resulted in this work. This book looks at how the brain works and goes through all the different areas of cogitation and distills four key aspects of thinking that will help you address any problem or study any subject matter that you wish to tackle. This book will open your mind to effective thinking tools. It will fill your mental toolbox with many specialized techniques for different thinking tasks. Just as a mechanic uses different tools specialized for different jobs, each of the aspects of thinking requires specializing thinking tools.

I was born in Syosset, New York and grew up in South Bend, Indiana in the USA. I graduated with my Master of Electrical Engineering at Purdue University and Ph.D. in Operations Research at Walden with a dissertation on Manifold Wireless networks. I have travelled to 30 countries and was the 2008 Heroclix World Champion (a chess-like game). I worked at General Electric Medical systems as a software engineer, working on Ultrasound and Magnetic Resonance Imaging. I joined Lucent Technologies in November 1996 as a software engineer working on 2G (TDMA). It became Alcatel-Lucent in 2007 and merged with Nokia in 2016. I have worked on 3G (UMTS) and 4G (LTE). I am currently (2019) a Systems Engineering working on architecting 5G Base Stations and ONAP. I have three USA granted patents #8,755,805 (USA Patent No. 8,755,805 B2, 2014), #7,443,804 (USA Patent No. 7,443,804 B2, 2008), and #9,918,232 (United States of America Patent No. 9,918,232, 2018) and numerous patents pending. I have published four books before this one: 32 Innovation Factors (Cheung, 32 Innovation Factors, 2003), 3G Cellular Systems in 90 minutes (Cheung, 3G Cellular Systems in 90 Minutes, 2003), Robotics in 90 minutes (Cheung, Robotics in 90 minutes, 2005), Renewable systems in 90 minutes (Cheung, Renewable Systems in 90 Minutes, 2005). You can visit my personal website   at   http://cheung.interzone.com

Part I – The Four Elements of Thinking

Chapter 1 – Introduction

Thinking produces success in life. All accomplishments are sparked with a single a thought. Your thoughts generate your aspirations resulting in your accomplishments. Developing your thinking skills, forges your destiny. The mind is a versatile instrument capable of tackling a variety of challenges. The basic mental faculties include: curiosity, consciousness, concentration, contemplation, dreaming, emotion, experience, facial recognition, imagination, instinct, interpreting sensations, intuition, language, listening, memory creation, memory retrieval, motor control, observation, pattern recognition, perception, personality expression, self-awareness, and willpower. The most remarkable ability of the brain is that the mind is a tool capable of altering itself.

From these basic mental tools arise the higher mental capabilities. These more advanced mental tools include abstraction, analysis, assessment, association, calculation, categorization, common sense, communication, comparison, comprehension, conceptual thought, conjecture, contrast, creativity, decision-making, deduction, elaboration, estimation, evaluation, extrapolation, generalization, induction, information processing, inquiry, interpretation, investigation, judgment, learning, logic, meta-learning, organization, persuasion, planning, prediction, problem solving, procedural knowledge, reading, reflection, reasoning, rhetoric, sapience, scrutiny, self-evaluation, speculation, strategizing, synthesis, understanding, and visualization. Mental processes join to overcome a problem or settle on a decision. These complex mental capabilities require mental prowess. Applied thinking enlists these mental capacities.

The mental tools and higher mental capabilities are the building blocks of this book. These components are grouped together to form four basic elements of thinking. The four elements of thinking represent four key aspects of thinking. They can be employed in any thinking activity with the most basic usage for problem solving. Chapter 23 presents an efficient way to solve problems using the Four elements. The four elements of thinking are: reasoning, creativity, synthesis, and evaluation. They break down the thinking process into four distinct elements, each one representing a key aspect of thinking.

1. ***Reasoning*** - Reasoning is thinking that is coherent and logical. This book will concentrate on four components of reasoning: inductive reasoning, deductive reasoning, abductive reasoning, and gathering evidence. Inductive reasoning is the act of drawing conclusions based on evidence, or from a set of premises (Copi, Cohen, & Flage, 2007). Deductive reasoning is drawing specific conclusions from general or universal premises (Terrell, 1967). Abductive reasoning is thinking that uses the available evidence to draw a reasonable conclusion (McKaughan, 2008). Gathering evidence and processing information is vital for all the other thinking activities. From the mental toolkit and higher order mental capabilities, reasoning involves abstraction, analysis, calculation, comparison, conceptual thought, deduction, evaluation, induction, information processing, investigation, logic, memory retrieval, observation, problem solving, and reasoning (Hurley, 2011).

2. ***Creativity*** - Creativity is the mental capacity to produce original ideas and forge new insights. This book will focus on the four pillars of creativity: insight, innovation, incubation, and investigation. Insight fosters observation and depth of understanding. Innovation is used to generate ideas and alternatives. Incubation entails deliberate and persistent contemplation. Investigation is purposeful and experimental creativity. Creativity is characterized by imagination, divergent thinking, idiosyncrasies, innovation, originality, and lateral thinking. From the higher order mental capabilities, creativity involves curiosity, contemplation, dreaming, elaboration, experience, extrapolation, imagination, instinct, interpreting sensations, intuition, language, learning, listening, memory retrieval, observation, reflection, speculation, and visualization (Koestler, 1964).

3. ***Synthesis*** - Synthesizing ideas together are the cross fertilization and bridging of concepts. Synthesis allows you to organize and classify things. This book highlights four components of synthesis thinking: linking, perspective, synthesis, and pivots. Linking is the ability to associate elements and to find patterns. Perspective is developing the ability to create a mental framework and find context. Synthesis is the ability to bridge concepts, cross-fertilize, and compare things. Pivots are the essential and crucial aspect of thing. With synthesis thinking you will isolate relevant patterns, identify the big picture, create meaningful structures, and recognize pivotal elements. Synthesis involves abstraction, analysis, categorization,

comparison, conceptual thought, contrast, elaboration, evaluation, experience, information processing, organization, pattern recognition, perception, planning, and strategizing (Gharajedgaghi, 2005).

4. *Evaluation* – Evaluation is the systematic determination of the worth and significance of a thing using criteria. This book will develop four components of evaluation: decisions, judgment, contingency, and validity. Decision-making is a crucial skill to select among viable alternatives. Judgment involves making sensible conclusions based on good reasoning. Contingency plans allow you to be adaptable and prepare for things that might go wrong. Validity is the ability to assess the truth of knowledge. Evaluation involves contemplating tradeoffs, identifying shortcomings, objective assessment, shrewd appraisal, systematic analysis, challenging conclusions, and testing assumptions to judge ideas, refining proposals and objective decision-making. Evaluation involves comparison, contrast, decision making, deduction, experience, induction, information processing, inquiry, interpretation, investigation, judgment, observation, and sapience (Van Gundy, 1988).

Each of these four principle aspects of thinking are explored with the goal of developing them as skills. Rational thought will become ordered and precise. Creative thought will be fostered. Synthesis thinking allows you to see the big picture. Evaluation skills make you focused and decisive. Each of these four aspects of thinking are associated with one of the classical four elements making them easy to remember and apply. The ancient Greek elements of earth, air, fire and water are infused in popular culture and have endured for eons since first proposed by Empedocles (490-430 BC) (Simplicius, 2011) and Plato (Plato, 360 BC).

1. *Earth Thinking* – Reasoning and logic shall be represented by the term *Earth thinking*. This term symbolizes a solid foundation for thinking. Earth Thinking is used as a mnemonic, a memory device, to remind you to ground your thinking in the techniques of reasoning and logic. The term was chosen because reasoning is one of the elemental aspects of thinking, and it was one of the elements used by the ancient Greeks to understand their world.

2. *Air Thinking* – Creativity and lateral thinking is represented by the term *Air Thinking*. Air was chosen to represent the adaptive, expansive, flowing, and ethereal nature of creativity. This mnemonic device will remind you to incorporate

the techniques of creativity on your thinking journeys. Air thinking is used to generate original ideas, proposals, solutions, and alternatives. It encourages you to think outside of the box. Air thinking gets you to search for alternative solutions. Its purpose is to stimulate creativity to assist in finding a viable solution when there appears to be none.

3. *Water Thinking* – Synthesizing concepts is represented by the term *Water Thinking*. This aspect of thinking represents associative, fluid, and immersive thinking. The memory device will encourage you to cross-fertilize ideas, bridge concepts, find pivots, and think in terms of the big picture. The Water element of thinking is used to find important links between key concepts in your problem. The goal of Water thinking is to find unifying associations, identify connecting concepts, and highlight the big picture. Synthesis thinking is used to break down a problem into its essential components and find critical links between those components. It makes the problem manageable by decomposing it. Problems that are compartmentalized can be tackled piecemeal. By isolating parts of the problem, one aspect can be analyzed at a time.

4. *Fire Thinking* – Evaluation, contingency planning, judgment, and decision making are represented by *Fire Thinking*. This aspect of thinking is used to represent thinking that can burn away irrelevancies. The word "fire" is used as a memory device to remind you to identify tradeoffs, and to assess objectively. Fire Thinking employs techniques to judge ideas and refine proposals. Fire thinking is used to refine proposed solutions. It allows you to objectively evaluate proposals through decision and selection criteria. You explore each alternative and select the best one. Evaluative thinking coaxes you to objectively identify flaws to refine proposals, critique suggestions, and select alternatives. Evaluative thinking can assess ideas for their effectiveness and further refine your candidate solutions.

Each of the four elements of thinking is comprised of four component skills. The secret to productive thinking is to apply these disciplines in your thinking endeavors.

1. *Earth Thinking* – Earth thinking represents reasoning and logic. It is composed of these four component skills:

Evidence – Gathering and processing information will form the basis of your reasoning efforts. Facts, opinions, and observations create a foundation upon which to draw conclusions. The ability to observe, record, gather, classify, and process facts plays a vital role in act of reasoning.

Inductive reasoning – Inductive reasoning develops generalized principles from detailed facts. General assertions and hypotheses are developed from specific examples.

Deductive reasoning – This is reasoning from the general to the particular; from cause to effect. Starting from a set of premises and specific examples, a conclusion is deduced.

Abductive reasoning – Infers reasonable conclusions from the available evidence. This type of reasoning goes from observation to a hypothesis that accounts for all the available and reliable facts.

2. *Air Thinking* – Air thinking represents creativity.

Investigation – Exploration and broad study to build a foundation of knowledge. Curiosity, exploration, inspection, inquiry, examination, and experimentation are the hallmarks of investigation. Building depth of knowledge on a topic spurs creativity because you can envision possibilities.

Incubation – Incubation is persistent and deliberate application of creative thought upon a problem. Creative incubation uses contemplation, careful preparation, and immersive study to nurture ideas to hatch. The incubation period is the time between your exposure to a problem or a subject and your development of a solution or idea.

Insight – Insight is the process of making a creative leap to a solution. This skill encourages you to gain a deep intuitive understanding of a problem.

Innovation – Innovation is the act of creating something that is unique, and original. Innovation encompasses methods which will deliberately generate new ideas and solutions.

3. *Water Thinking* – Water thinking represents associative thinking. It is composed of the following four component skills and abilities:

Linking – This is the skill to find relationships and patterns between things or situations. Finding connections between concepts reduces a complex problem into manageable parts. Identifying meaningful associations helps to structure your thinking.

Perspective – Perspective is the ability to create a framework for thinking. Perspective is the ability to see trends and understand the overall context of the problem. The ability to place things into a greater context and environment allows you to develop a gestalt.

Synthesis – Synthesis is the ability to compare, contrast and combine things. This component involves the combination of two things to create something new. A holistic synthesis is characterized by the comprehension of intimately interconnected parts and to see how they could form a whole.

Pivots – Pivots are the key aspect of a system. This is the ability to recognize a vital element in a problem. Pivots are also turning points in a situation or series of events. Identifying pivots entails finding the keystone of a problem or subject.

4. *Fire Thinking* – Fire thinking represents evaluation.

Decision – Decision making as a skill used to make intelligent choices. Identifying goals, constraints, alternatives, criteria, consequences are vital to this process. Then, decision-making selection techniques can be used.

Judgment – Judgment is the objective assessment of a situation or proposed solutions to a problem. Judgment coaxes you to confidently arrive at objective, wise, and reasonable conclusions. Good judgment is a cornerstone of assessment and evaluation.

Contingency – Developing contingency plans and alternatives is achieved by understanding vulnerabilities, hazards, and anticipating failure. Identifying proper responses to hazards is the basis for creating contingencies that allow you to adapt to threats. Failure to plan is a plan for failure. Preparing for the unexpected mitigates emergencies and accidents.

Validity – Developing the skills to be able to ascertain the truth of a matter. Validity involves determining the reliability, and credibility of information.

The following table summarizes the four key components of each of the elements of thinking. As you practice each skill or ability, they will become second nature to you.

ELEMENT OF THINKING	COMPONENT	DESCRIPTION
EARTH (Reasoning)	Evidence	Gathering, recording, classifying, and assessing facts to create a foundation for conclusions and exploration.
EARTH	Inductive Reasoning	Reasoning from the particular to the general by developing principles from specific facts.
EARTH	Deductive Reasoning	Reasoning from the general to the particular by starting from premises and ending with a conclusion.
EARTH	Abductive Reasoning	Drawing reasonable conclusions from the available evidence through a hypothesis that accounts for all the available and reliable facts.
AIR (Creativity)	Investigation	Building a foundation of knowledge through curiosity, exploration, inspection, inquiry, examination, and experimentation.
AIR	Incubation	The persistent and deliberate application of creative thought upon a problem through contemplation, preparation, and immersive study. The incubation period is the time between the exposure to a problem to the development of a solution or idea.
AIR	Insight	The process of making a creative leap to a solution spurred from a deep intuitive understanding of a problem.
AIR	Innovation	The deliberate act of creating unique, and original ideas and solutions.
WATER (Synthesis)	Linking	Finding connections, relationships and patterns between concepts or situations reducing a complex problem into manageable parts.
WATER	Perspective	The creation of a framework for thinking or a gestalt using trending, greater context, and

		the environment.
WATER	Synthesis	Comparing, contrasting and combining to achieve comprehension by understanding how interconnected parts form a whole.
WATER	Pivots	Finding the key aspect or recognizing the most vital element in a problem.
FIRE (Evaluation)	Decision	Making tradeoffs and identifying selection criteria to make intelligent choices.
FIRE	Judgment	Arriving at objective, wise, and reasonable conclusions through assessment and evaluation.
FIRE	Contingency	Developing contingency plans by understanding vulnerabilities, hazards, and developing responses to adapt to changing circumstances.
FIRE	Validation	Ascertaining the truth of a matter by testing for reliability, and credibility of information.

Table 1 - Elements of Thinking Components

Viewed as skills, each of the four elements of thinking can be improved through training. Each of four components that comprise the elements of thinking can be honed. The brain should be exercised, just as an athlete physically trains.

The four elements of thinking will guide you to methodically think through problems, make decisions, synthesize concepts, generate solutions, and evaluate proposals. You will examine your thinking and develop better thinking habits.

Chapter 2 – Earth Thinking and Reasoning

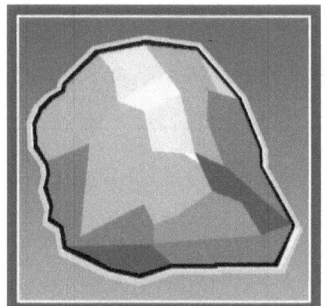 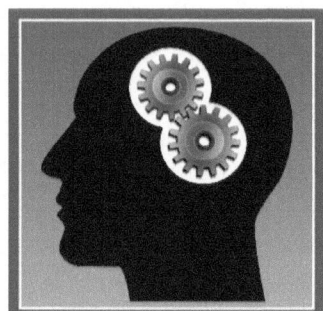

The Earth element represents critical thinking and logical reasoning. Critical thinking is the application of reason and logic in structured thought. Critical thinking is also known as structured thinking. Applied logic, calculation, deduction, formal logic, induction, abduction, and meta-logic are the building blocks of logical reasoning (Hurley, 2011). These building blocks shape thinking as an architect would create a structure from the ground up. The Earth element of thinking buttresses analysis using logic. Earth thinking structures your thinking so that you can develop solutions based on solid reasoning. The rules of logic provide the earthen-works as a foundation to base your arguments upon. Earth Thinking is comprised of evidence, inductive reasoning, deductive reasoning, and abductive reasoning.

In addition to basic mental tools, simple down to earth questions will serve as the foot soldiers for marshaling reason and logic. The basic investigative questions are: Who? What? Where? When? Why? How? To what degree? and, Is that true? These questions applied at the proper pivot points will act as levers to magnify the force of your thinking. Continued probing will unearth more terra incognita. Some simple analytical questions include: Why is that true? When does that occur? What makes that so? Why is that so? How does that work? Who can make that happen?

What caused that to happen? What proof do you have? Where did you find the evidence? Use these inquiry questions to give your thinking solid footing.

Evidence – The basis of any sort of reasoning is facts, data, and evidence. Gathering evidence by marshalling your powers of observation and employing investigative questions. The four principles of the evidence component are: identifying assumptions, gathering information, organizing evidence, and assessment. In the process of coming to reasonable conclusions, making intelligent decisions, and discourse with others, having accurate information will give your thinking a solid foundation to work from.

Deductive reasoning – This is the act of proceeding from general principles to the understanding of the specifics (Terrell, 1967). Deduction is a thinking process that can be learned. It employs a body of general knowledge to identify logical consequences. A relevant principle, fact, or rule is selected. You then apply that rule to a specific aspect of your problem. You can develop important conclusions by using this process. Deductive reasoning leads to valuable insights that often cannot be reached by any other method. A doctor can deduce a diagnosis by drawing from a body of medical knowledge. As a systems engineer working in a high technology industry, I solve numerous problems every day. I use engineering principles to deduce how a new wireless system design should proceed.

Inductive reasoning – Inductive thinking finds premises that support the conclusion in a way that it is improbable that the conclusion would be false if the premises are true (Copi, Cohen, & Flage, 2007). *Deduction* works from the general to the specific. By contrast, *induction* proceeds from the specifics to the general. Given a sufficient body of evidence one can derive general rules that apply to a group of things. Science uses induction to determine natural laws based on experiments and evidence. Induction harvests facts to grow a body of knowledge. This knowledge provides the foundation for making a reliable generalization. A hypothesis of what might be true is formed because of calculated reasoning. The hypothesis can then be accepted, tested, rejected, verified, and refined. Eventually, a sufficient body of facts transforms theory into knowledge. Inductive reasoning is used by scientists to fashion a rule through evidence and observation.

Abductive reasoning – This term was first introduced by Charles Sanders Peirce, an American philosopher (Peirce, 1992). This is a form of logical inference which tries to arrive at a reasonable conclusion through the available evidence. In abductive reasoning, unlike deductive reasoning, the premises do not guarantee a conclusion. This type of reasoning shines in the disciplines of law, computer science, diagnosticians, detectives, and artificial intelligence research.

Earth thinking employs deduction, induction, abduction, inquiry questions, and evidence gathering in thinking. An essential part of thinking through a problem is to apply critical thinking. Once you become accustomed to applying the tools of structured thinking to your problem, you will find your ideas rooted in sound reasoning. Earth thinking serves as a metaphor to remind you to dig up evidence, to entrench your work in reason, ground your thinking in logic, and buttress your thinking with structured arguments.

The problem-solving journey is a step-by-step process. Breaking down the effort allows you to focus on one step at a time. Each step becomes a manageable thought exercise. The four elements of thinking form a thinking process. The Earth element of thinking is an integral part of that process, contributing logic and reason to the mix. The Air element of thinking generates options and ideas. Earth thinking takes those new ideas and gives them a logical and practical basis. Water thinking serves to find connections and context. Then, Earth thinking can use those connections in the inductive and deductive process. Fire thinking applies evaluation, decision making, and judgment. Earth thinking lends a logical basis for those evaluations.

At the start of your thinking journey, Earth thinking lays the groundwork through the development of a thesis. The thesis defines the problem statement. Crafting a problem statement and identifying the key aspects of the problem generates a foundation to work from. You then dig for relevant facts. Gathering, organizing, and evaluating relevant information produces the building blocks for the analysis. Inquiry questions will help you dig deeper into the problem.

Earth thinking creates logical chains of thought to arrive at sound conclusions. You identify the underlying assumptions, refine the premises, chart the situation, use induction, develop a hypothesis, and apply deductive reasoning. Critical thinking strives to reason through your problem.

Earth thinking, or Critical Thinking, is concerned with creating and evaluating logical chains of thought. This allows you to explore ideas and refine potential solution. Critical thinking helps you arrive at sound conclusions. The component chapters (6 through 9) describe techniques for Critical Thinking and detail the principles for applying induction, deduction and abductive thinking. Earth thinking components give you down-to-earth methods to solidify your deductive and inductive skills.

In the following chapters each of the components of Earth thinking (evidence, inductive reasoning, deductive reasoning, and abductive reasoning) will be explored. The following table summarizes those chapters by describing the component and its associated central principles and concepts. Each of these principles plays a vital role in developing a better comprehension of that component.

EARTH THINKING		
COMPONENT	DESCRIPTION	PRINCIPLES
Evidence	Gathering, recording, classifying, and processing facts to create a foundation for conclusions.	Assumptions Gathering evidence Organizing information Assessing
Inductive Reasoning	Reasoning from the particular to the general by developing principles from specific facts	Evidence Generalization Hypothesis Experiment Scientific Method Conclusions
Deductive Reasoning	Reasoning from the general to the particular by starting from premises and ending with a conclusion	Formal Logic Argument Syllogism Premise Assumption Conclusion
Abductive Reasoning	Drawing reasonable conclusions from the available evidence through a hypothesis that accounts for all the available and reliable facts	Causality Occam's Razor Decomposition Simplicity How & Why Conclusion

Table 2 - Earth Thinking Component & Principles

Chapter 3 – Air Thinking and Creativity

The Air element of thinking represents creativity. The creative aspect of thinking is a unique and vital human endowment. Creativity is the capability to make leaps of insight, spur curiosity, produce novel solutions, generate ideas, and harness intuition. Each of these aspects of creativity is examined. Numerous techniques have been developed to bolster creative thinking through the ages. This book will provide some techniques to help you foster creatively. The goal of the Air element of thinking is to generating ideas and solutions. The Air element of thinking represents the production phase of thinking. Good thinkers produce a large quantity of high-quality ideas. They can conceptualize problems in various ways. They produce effective solutions and responses to deal with problems. Good thinkers see a problem from different perspectives, use a variety of invention methods, actively seek ideas, adopt different investigative approaches, take intellectual risks, entertain unusual ideas, break with conformity, and also suspend judgment (Koestler, 1964).

It is important not to eliminate proposals when applying the Air element of thinking. Elimination is the job of the Fire element of thinking. The Air element of thinking generates solutions, and the Fire element of thinking burns away unfeasible proposals. Because it is often necessary to put forward provocative ideas, you need suspend judgment during the idea generation phase. New ideas are like freshly laid eggs. Both are fragile and require protection. The beginning is the most fragile period time for a hatchling idea. Creativity often runs counter to the natural habits of recognition, judgment and criticism. The brain is a pattern recognition engine that condemns things that do fit established patterns. Creativity involves mental provocation, exploration and risk taking.

As with all the elements of thinking, the symbol of Air is a mental reminder for you to step through each of the major aspects of thinking. By doing so, you will learn to look at problems from many vantage points to facilitate a good solution. You will be able to evaluate and judge ideas using Fire thinking. With the Air element of thinking, you will harness your powers of creative thinking. It might be true that some people are more creative than others. But ultimately, some people have more tools in their creative toolbox. Creativity is a blend of talent, method, training, and skill. The key insight is that you can develop your creativity skill. If you do not, you are at the mercy of just your innate creative capability. Make creativity a regular part of your thinking process.

The Air element of thinking is composed of four components which capture some of the key aspects of fostering creativity. The four components are: investigation, incubation, insight, and innovation.

1. **INVESTIGATION** – Investigation involves exploration and curiosity. To be creative, one must deeply explore a subject. Expertise are developed by thorough investigation and study. One should strive to learn everything they can about the object of inquiry. One should seek out articles, books, research, lectures, and artifacts that comprise the existing body of knowledge on your subject of interest. The more background and expertise that you develop the more ideas you will be able to generate.

2. **INCUBATION** – Incubation is the process of allowing your mind to gestate upon a problem. Directed mental activities, such as contemplation and meditation can be used. Your mind will also unconsciously work on a problem if you are persistent. Investigation and incubation are complementary aspects of Air thinking. Many problems are solved by perseverance. Rumination allows you to arrive at insightful ideas over time. Creative inspiration can ebb and flow. Build a solid foundation of understanding through investigation and stimulate your mind into work on the problem subconsciously.

3. **INSIGHT** – Insight is discovering some aspect of your problem that was not originally obvious. It means seeing what everyone else saw and thinking what no

one else thought. It is the "*Aha!*" moment in problem solving. Creativity thrives on insight. To gain insight use your intuition, mental flexibility, mental fluency and use comparisons. Intuition is the ability to understand something without conscious thought. Mental fluency is ease of cognition. Flexibility is the ability to think in new ways. Comparison can also generate insight.

4. **INNOVATION** – Innovation is idea generation which is a defining aspect of creativity. Innovation is the development of an original solution to a problem. Innovation involves generating ideas through deliberate methods such as brainstorming, collaborative creativity, innovation factors and visualization. Investigation, incubation, insight and innovation are the yeast that keeps creativity in active fermentation.

Creativity has seven aspects: (1) Curiosity (2) Intuition (3) Insight (4) Perspective (5) Deconditioning (6) Unconventional thinking (7) Innovation factors.

1. **CURIOSITY** – Curiosity is a natural experience. Thinking, living, higher order life is naturally hardwired to be curious. Curiosity is a thirst for understanding. To achieve the highest level of actualization, people strive to leave a legacy. People are driven to be unique and express ourselves creatively. No two things in nature are identical. Even identical twins are different. Humans derive satisfaction from creative thought and action. We want to be unique, express ourselves, and bestow our own sense of individuality in the world (Lieberman, 2006). Curiosity is an important part of the *investigation* part of Air thinking.

2. **INTUITION** – Intuition is educated guessing. One human endowment is making a smart guess to identify a potential solution. Intuition is that voice in your mind guiding your thinking. It is a mental beacon cutting through the darkness. Intuition is taking a mental leap. Creativity is spurred on by intuition. Intuition uses your body of personal knowledge mixed with your experience to generate a viable solution to a problem. Experience develops your intuition about a subject. Intuition is employed in the *Insight* aspect of Air thinking.

3. **INSIGHT** – Insight is discovering some aspect of your problem that was not originally obvious. Insight is one of the four aspects of the Air element of thinking.

4. **PERSPECTIVE** – Perspective is part and parcel of the Water element of thinking. The Water element of thinking seeks to develop perspective on your

problem. Perspective is developing a broader view. It is understanding the context, environment and big picture. Perspective encourages creativity because an understanding of your environment opens options which produces ideas. Perspective is one of the four parts of Water thinking.

5. **DECONDITIONING** – Deconditioning is escaping from mental shackles. Creativity requires you to escape the pull of existing patterns, and familiar habits. Creativity smashes through mental roadblocks by finding a better way to do things. The air element of thinking provides a mechanism to deliberately engage in creative thought. Your mind will dance with new ideas. Air thinking is concerned with replacing existing patterns; escaping past experiences and shifting perspectives. We spend much of our lives developing experiences, building up our common sense, laying down patterns. We need these patterns to get through life. The brain is wired to make and use patterns. However, our existing notions, hardened attitudes, established patterns, idioms, stubborn opinions, symbolic systems, and beliefs imprison our thinking. They lock in and confine our ability to think outside the box. Air thinking eliminates these barriers to creativity. People get trapped into doing things a certain way. They perform tasks a certain way because of conditioning. Cultural traditions exemplify this.

6. **UNCONVENTIONAL THINKING** – Unconventional thinking is the willingness to think about the unexpected. This type of thinking stresses unusual, unique, and original solutions. Novel uses for common objects can be found, using them for purposes other than their original design. Air thinking urges you to continue to look for alternatives that might be better than the solution you had first identified. Most problems have alternate solutions that also get you to your destination but optimize different constraints from other ones. There is often more than one way to do things, more than one way to skin a problem, more than one way to think about a situation, and more than one way to look at a problem. Acknowledging, identifying and searching for alternatives are fundamental to creativity.

7. **IDEA GENERATION** – There are four ways ideas are typically generated: exploration, contemplation, serendipity, and similarity. These four ways correspond to the investigation, incubation, insight, and innovation aspect of Air thinking respectively.

Creativity is defined as having or showing imagination and artistic or intellectual inventiveness (Webster's New World Dictionary, 1984). It often stimulates the imagination and inventive powers. Creativity is characterized by originality, expressiveness, and imagination (Webster's New World Dictionary, 1984). The Macquarie Dictionary defines "*creative*" as generative, ground-breaking, innovative, original, or hand-made. The Encyclopedia Britannica defines creativity as the ability to make or otherwise bring into existence something new, whether a new solution to a problem, a new method or device, or a new artistic object or form (Encyclopedia Britannica, Founded 1768).

There are four general ways of achieving a creative solution (Mednick, 1962):

1. **FLUENCY** – Mental fluency is utilizing your thinking prowess. Intuition, mental flexibility, adaptability, and serendipity are all bolstered with mental fluency. Intuition is unconscious reasoning. Mental adaptability allows you to produce original ideas based on changing circumstances. Serendipity is stumbling upon a solution while searching for something else.

2. **SIMILARITY** – Another common path to a creative solution is similarity. The use of adaptation, analogy, comparison, paradigm shifts, and translation are mechanisms by which similarity can be used to achieve innovative solutions. These mechanisms adapt a solution of one a problem to a different one. This method reuses a successful solution to a problem in a different way. Thus, it generates an original solution when applied to a new situation. Comparison (similarity & difference) is a principle in the *insight* component of Air thinking.

3. **CONTEMPLATION** - Another mechanism by which creativity is realized is through meditation and contemplation. Willpower and rational contemplation can spur creativity. Relaxation, meditation, contemplation are ways to incubate ideas. Intentional contemplation is a methodical way to produce innovative solutions. This mechanism differs from the other methods because this is a premeditated search for ideas. Meditative creativity does not rely on luck (serendipity), nor does it recycle existing ideas (similarity). This mechanism paves its own way by intentionally generating original ideas. Contemplation is a principle of the *incubation* component of Air thinking.

4. **EXPLORATION** - The exploration method uses methodical experimentation. This method uses different approaches until a solution is found. Consider a chef

that tries different spices, cooking methods, and ingredients. The cook tries a variety of combinations until an appealing dish is generated. In this technique, the inventor methodically tries permutations of things related to the problem. In the case of the chef, he might step through his supply of different spices.

There are four things that foil creative thinking:

1. **JUDGMENT** - Judgment is used by people to narrow our selection or analysis of something. However, judgment hinders the breaking of old patterns to deliberately find a new pattern. Thus, it is important to suspend judgment when trying to think laterally and creatively. Judgment is an important aspect of thinking. Thus, it is employing in Fire thinking. Without it, refining ideas would be difficult. Air thinking generates new ideas. Fire thinking evaluates and refines proposals. Judgment often incinerates an idea prematurely.

2. **BIAS** - Preconceptions, beliefs, and biases that someone has going into a situation affects how they will see the situation. Often, a person will look for data, and viewpoints that back up their entrenched beliefs. Preconceived notions make it difficult for you to see the world in a different light. To be creative, you must have an open mind to see the situation from a different perspective. This requires you to be aware of your biases on the matter. Some predispositions have a rational basis while others have been handed down through parents, society, stories and myths. One should allow their notions to be questioned. Allow ideas to stand trial against the test of reason. That will open the gateway to creativity.

3. **CLASSIFICATION** - The mind classifies things to make sense out of the world. When one perceives an object or learns of an idea they tend to classify it into some existing category in the mind. However, in so doing they do not give a new idea the latitude it needs to establish a unique conceptual identity. This classification effect hinders lateral thinking on a new notion that has not been encountered before.

4. **FAMILIAR PATTERNS** – The mind is good at abstraction. The right side of the brain is good at seeing whole patterns. Randomly select six different pictures. Now, find four ways to group those six things. You will discover that people will find numerous ways to group a random collection of images. The grouping, patterns, abstractions, and classifications that we hold in our mind allow us to make predictions about how things will behave in certain situations. It allows

us to navigate the complexities of life. Useful insights are discovered by using patterns. The familiar patterns that we want to see in a situation may limit our ability to spot new and unfamiliar patterns.

The air symbol serves as a mnemonic to use the techniques of creativity. These techniques will enhance your creative abilities. Developing a habit of seeking originality and applying your creative endowments is the objective of air thinking. Deliberately using creativity will generate solutions and expand your thinking.

AIR THINKING		
COMPONENT	**DESCRIPTION**	**PRINCIPLES**
Investigation	Building a foundation of knowledge through curiosity, examination, experimentation, exploration, and inquiry.	Curiosity Examination Experimentation Exploration Inquiry
Incubation	The persistent and deliberate application of creative thought upon a problem through contemplation, preparation, and immersive study. The incubation period is the time between the exposure to a problem to the development of a solution or idea	Breaking Conditioning Contemplation Eureka Effect Problem Reformulation Unconventional Thinking
Insight	The process of making a creative leap to a solution spurred from a deep intuitive understanding of a problem	Flexibility Intuition Mental Fluency Comparison (Similarity & Difference)
Innovation	The deliberate act of creating unique, and original ideas and solutions	Brainstorm Collaborative Creativity Gedanken Innovation Factors Visualization

Table 3 - Air Thinking Components & Principles

Chapter 4 – Water Thinking and Synthesis

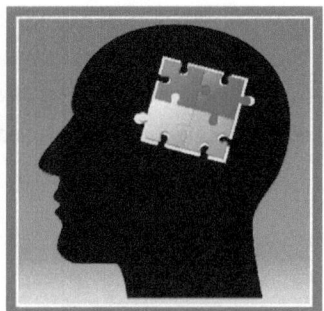

The aspect of thinking represented by Water is synthesis thinking. Synthesizing ideas involves linking them together through association. The objective of the Water element of thinking is to find meaningful associations and identifying the big picture. As mental associations are developed, patterns will emerge. Water thinking integrates ideas together. The act of synthesizing ideas results in a better understanding of the context of the problem. A "big picture" perspective of the problem will emerge from your efforts (Gharajedgaghi, 2005).

There are four components that characterize Water thinking: Linking, Perspective, Synthesis, and Pivots.

1. **LINKING** – The hallmark of Water thinking is to integrate ideas together with the objective of gaining insight and a greater perspective of the system. You need to be tolerant of conflicting ideas. Water thinking facilitates the linking of ideas in an objective manner. At the heart of Water thinking is to find connections to understand the system, gain greater perspective which will inspire new solutions. Through this enhanced understanding, you will see hidden patterns and gain a greater view of context and environment of the system.

2. **PERSPECTIVE** – When you step back, you can see the forest through the trees. Perspective comes when you can see the city through the skyscrapers. While

close to the ground we see fields, and rivers. In the sky, you can see that the earth is a sphere. When you assemble a jigsaw puzzle, a big picture emerges from the pieces. Life is full of hidden patterns. Perspective is broadly seeing linkages between systems.

3. **SYNTHESIS** – The synthesis of two things is another aspect of Water thinking. Many key developments in history have synthesized two systems together. Many landmark inventions resulted from the synthesis of ideas. Many successful technologies resulted from the synthesis of ideas.

4. **PIVOTS** –Not all events are created equal. Some developments, events, ideas, and creations are more important to us than others. Most systems have critical points where small events can potentially have great impact. You will gain invaluable insight by learning how to identify pivotal root causes. Pivotal ideas start a domino of events whose repercussions echo through time. The actions and ideas of some people create important watershed moments. Pivots are important to understand to gain a greater perspective and context on a situation which creates a foundation of knowledge to build solutions from (Gladwell, 2002).

Finding patterns is the basis of the pivots component of Water thinking. You gather data, make observations, use analytical thinking, find patterns in the data, and then organize it. This allows someone to discover important trends or gain insight into a problem. Knowledge alone will not produce a solution. To employ knowledge requires finding useful patterns and relationships in relevant data. Patterns are meaningful in context. Some patterns are significant in one context but irrelevant in another. The best insights will come when you can discern the forest from the individual trees. You need a broad perspective to see patterns, and yet work with individual elements that make up the pattern.

A holistic approach can be used in thinking. In a system, everything is connected to the other elements of the system in some way. To gain full understanding, one needs to look at the total context. It is helpful to look at relationships with a broad perspective. By identifying relationships between elements of a system, a greater context can be developed. This approach will assist you in evaluating pros and cons of a problem or advantages and disadvantages of a situation. When you understand the broad context, you can assess the ramification of decisions.

For the synthesis aspect of water thinking, any type of idea can be integrated together, not just for producing inventions. Synthesizing concepts has been used nearly every endeavor that Man has engaged in. Many important discoveries have been made through interdisciplinary sciences. Universities offer interdisciplinary degrees that combine two fields of study together.

Water thinking can be applied to ordinary events. The techniques work equally well on a synthesis of grand ideas as they do with the fusion of down-to-earth applications. The goal of Water thinking, is to get you synthesize ideas. First, you step back and look at your whole problem. You consider the data; and then look for things that can be used in conjunction with one another.

Water thinking encourages you to take the long-range view. The long-term view is part of the big picture perspective. Ask yourself the following questions: what will happen in the long run? What will be the impact of this proposal or idea in the future? What is the greater context of this problem or situation? What are the persistent issues? How might the system evolve? What are the ramifications over time?

One essential part of synthesis thinking is methodical perception. Good observation assists good thinking. Cultivating your skills of observation will help you find associations between concepts. Scrutiny and observation are valuable tools in your mental toolbox. Observation plays a vital role in identifying pivots, bottlenecks, trends, and frameworks.

Finding associations requires good observation. So, the first step to synthesizing ideas is to deliberately and systematically use the five senses to assess the problem. Moreover, you should hone, and develop your senses to their fullest potential (Gelb, 2000). You should analyze a problem using each of your senses. Take the time to carefully observe the relevant objects of the problem. Imagine that you are seeing it for the first time. Ask yourself who produced it? What function does the form suggest? What is unusual about this object? What distinctive visual features does it have? Where does it fit? Where was it produced? When was it made? Why does it have this structure? Why does it have the form that it does? Why was it made? How was it made? Was it produced by man or machine? Next, apply this same technique using your other senses.

Some problems are conceptual and have no physical form. The techniques employed by Water thinking are equally effective here. The key is to find relevant associations between concepts. Associations lead to emergent patterns. Emergent patterns allow you to identify associations, a greater perspective, trends, catalysts, bottlenecks and pivots. Thus, emergent patterns lead to greater understanding. Greater understanding helps you produce knowledge, ideas, and solutions.

Water thinking finds connections between concepts. You started by gathering evidence and organizing it. You can then find associations. Synthesis thinking identifies frameworks, strategies, and pivots. It surveys to give you the lay of the land for your mental expedition. Finding patterns is an ongoing process. New connections lead to new insights which lead to new associations. Water thinking uses synthesis to craft solutions. It inspires you to compare, contrast, cross-fertilize, and reformulate concepts (Gharajedgaghi, 2005). Sarnoff Mednick claimed creativity is based on associative thinking. Synthesis and association are critical in the creative process (Mednick, 1962).

Identifying the big picture is a hallmark of Water thinking. It represents the synthesis of major concepts into a governing framework. Synthesis thinking is about developing a grand strategy, game plan, frame of reference, idea ecology, gestalt, and holistic viewpoint. Strategy produces a vision, and central theme for your thinking efforts. You arrive at these vantage points by pinpointing connections between relevant concepts. When a commander surveys a battlefield, he devises a strategy. He sees patterns in the organization of troops and equipment. Like a symphony conductor, the essence of his job is to see the big picture. His conceptual framework encompasses linkages between the tools at his disposal.

Diametrically opposed ideas (a thesis and antithesis) can be synthesized to form an original idea. Differing viewpoints are the source of compromise, creativity, and cross-fertilization of ideas. When people voice conflicting viewpoints, they get the chance to synthesize their ideas together. This requires that you keep an objective frame of mind. Try to view the situation as a third-party observer might. Try to reserve judgment until you have considered the opposing opinions. Taking a third person perspective allows you to take a step back and see the big picture. Synthesis thinking is the process of reconciling different viewpoints. The key is to find a common starting point. This paves the way to integrate the two viewpoints.

Someone who has mastered a skill or subject will have more perspective than a beginner. They can see how the present situation relates to the overall system. Masters grasp how their actions influence the greater whole. The benefit of experience is depth of understanding. The water element of thinking cultivates an understanding of hubs, bottlenecks, trends, frameworks, ecologies and associations. The ability to craft connections enables you to see the big picture. You will see how your subject matter fits into a greater context. Water thinking cultivates the mind's ability to gain perspective. It deliberately looks for associations between major ideas. By applying Water thinking, you will train your mind to perceive the problem in a greater context, and thus gain a greater perspective. Making associations between ideas enables you to find underlying patterns (Barabasi, 2014).

WATER THINKING		
COMPONENT	**DESCRIPTION**	**PRINCIPLES**
Linking	Finding connections, relationships and patterns between concepts or situations reducing a complex problem into manageable parts.	Association Cross-Fertilization Decomposition Organization Patterns
Perspective	The creation of a framework for thinking or a gestalt using trending, greater context, and the environment.	Big Picture & Maps Ecology & System Framework Planning Viewpoint
Synthesis	Comparing, contrasting and combining to achieve comprehension by understanding how interconnected parts form a whole.	Compare & Contrast Conclusion & Summary Permutation & Combination Thesis & Antithesis Tradeoffs & Compromise
Pivots	Finding the key aspect or recognizing the most vital element in a problem.	Anchors Bottlenecks Catalyst Tipping Point Trend

Table 4 - Water Thinking Components & Principles

Chapter 5 – Fire Thinking and Evaluation

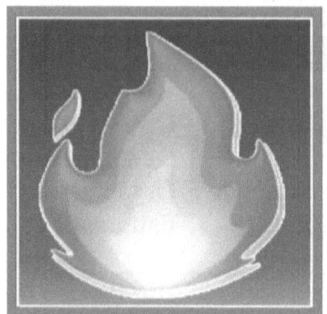 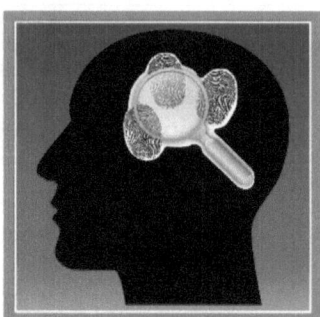

The aspect of thinking represented by the Fire Symbol is Evaluation. There are four aspects which characterize the Fire element of thinking: decision, judgment, contingency, and validity. Fire thinking also goes by other names: vertical thinking, adversarial thinking, contingency planning, and judgmental thinking. These four components of Fire thinking symbolize the evaluation process.

The Fire symbol was chosen to represent evaluative thinking because it can serve to objectively burn away the improper and irrelevant parts of a problem and proposed solutions.

Fire thinking is composed of four components: making decisions, creating contingencies, applying judgment, and testing for validity.

1. **JUDGMENT** – The Fire element of thinking uses good judgment in the evaluation process. Judgment involves careful review and critique of a proposal or project. The available evidence in the form of experience, testimony, facts, observations, facts, beliefs, and opinions are carefully considered. The merits and flaws of a plan or solution are analyzed. Extraneous elements and redundant parts can be eliminated. The key requirements will be defined and clarified. In this way, counter proposals, constructive criticism, and revisions can be suggested.

2. **DECISIONS** – The mind is a decision machine. It is constantly evaluating a myriad of inputs from your surroundings (Hoenig, 2000). It is capable of absorbing hundreds of facts and juggling them to arriving at a decision. Every choice we

make guides us into the future. Your destiny hinges on the choices that you make today. Living is making choices. What tasks should I perform today? What plans will I make? Where do I need to travel to? Who do I need to meet? These are just a few examples of decisions you commonly make. The mind often considers numerous alternatives when making those decisions. It quickly rejects some options and you mull over other choices. Observe how you make some of these decisions. You have already developed a process of evaluation that you might not be consciously aware of. The fire element of thinking will introduce you to techniques for decision making. Many things in the real world are not cut and dry, black and white. You must act based on the available facts, selection criteria, decision factors, tradeoffs, constraints, and requirements. You get a sense of the likelihood, or the probability that this solution will be effective. The air element of thinking will dream up creative possibilities. Fire thinking assesses the merits and flaws to each of those possibilities. Fire thinking gets you to assess, modify, refine, discard, or adopt candidate solutions. Fire thinking is the first step in turning potential ideas into kinetic action.

3. **CONTINGENCY** – The journey of life is filled with speed bumps, potholes, and pitfalls. Contingencies are a way to plan for unexpected and unforeseen circumstances that will invariably arise. Applying the techniques of Fire thinking get you to think about alternatives and fail-safes. This is done with the purpose of trying to refine a solution before eliminating it. It is often easy to kill a good idea before it has been fully hatched. The beginning is a very delicate time (Herbert, 1990). Fire thinking should be used to identify potential pitfalls with a solution, so that the solution can be refined. Contingency plans allow you to be flexible and adapt to changing circumstances. One of the goals of Fire thinking is to produce contingencies by anticipating detrimental situations and developing an appropriate response. Flaws can be addressed with a contingency plan. Producing a contingency plan is a deliberate strategy which allows your ideas to thrive in adversarial conditions.

4. **VALIDITY** – If one wants to know the truth and validate assertions they need to go to the sources, not the commentators (Barzun, May 15, 2001). To evaluate something objectively requires one to consciously set aside many of their biases, preconceptions, and engrained beliefs. One should strive to rationally evaluate a problem based only on pertinent facts, context, and reasoning. Ascertaining validity may require you to suspend what you were taught in school, parental

advice, cultural norms, religious views, and previous experiences. The mind is structured in such a way that it tends to hastily judge a situation base on inadequate details. This inertia of history is a powerful force. It is not without benefit. For the sake of survival, it allows you to make rapid decisions to save your life. If you had to carefully evaluate everything you did every day as a new situation you would hardly get anything accomplished. In fact, your brain has a dedicated rapid response center, the Amygdala. The aim of Fire thinking is to apply objective evaluation to problems under scrutiny. This is related to the fact that the mind is essentially an analog chemical-based computer. The white matter of your brain is a network of neurons whose connections are sculpted from your experiences. Memory and logic are smoothly integrated into an analog thinking system. The drawback is that the mind biases new inputs and situations based on previous history. The experiences and learning during your life establish a neutral landscape of connections (white matter) that filters incoming information against patterns, ideas, thoughts, experiences you have previously had. Objectivity requires that you consciously hold back the influence of your past learning and experiences so that you can effectively and impartially judge a new important (non-trivial) situation or problem.

Sometimes, we strive diligently to solve the wrong problem. Other times, we have appropriately identified the problem, but are going down the wrong path, developing an ineffective solution. Fire thinking gets a person to reevaluate a problem. In some cases, the goal must be changed, and in other cases a different alternative should be considered. Fire thinking eliminate irrelevant parts of your problem and ineffective parts of a solution.

Calculate the short-range and long-term payoffs. Consider the immediate effects of the proposal. Determine the immediate benefits and what the direct consequences will be. For the long-term, consider how the context, implementation, operation, and circumstances change over time. Assessing short-term effects will help you make objective evaluations because you rationally consider consequences. By understanding immediate environmental stressors, you can adapt a solution. By considering the long-term payoffs you will integrate broader trends and greater perspective into your thinking.

Emotions can come into play when thinking about a problem, or idea. Fire thinking does not reject an idea without reason. Acknowledge these feelings. Then, try to identify why someone feels a certain way about an idea. Emotions can help establish a valid counterpoint. Fire thinking seeks to identify valid counterpoints.

By addressing counterpoints and issues a better alterative can be produced, or a proposal can be refined. Use Fire thinking to find faults with the aim of steering towards a viable solution. Turn emotionally-based assessments into factually-based evaluations. When you identify faults, they should have a reasonable basis; they should make sense. You may feel something will not work, or that this other solution will work better. Identify reasons why you feel that way. Are there existing examples that have also failed? Are there facts that contradict the claim? Find a specific aspect of the problem that would improve the overall solution if that aspect were modified.

Learn to assess a situation tactically. Consider who has a vested interest in the problem. Determine what forces are at work. Consider what support and resources each side has. Assess how you can influence the interested parties. Find out who is opposed to the proposal. Identify who is in favor of the idea. What are the vested interests? What forces are operating in opposition to each other? What would neutralize or minimize opposing forces? What is the historical context of the situation? What are the conflicting interests? What would strengthen or augment their position? What options are available? What would be the reaction to those options? Are there contingency plans in place? What sort of plans are in place on either side? What resources do the opposing parties have? Who stands to gain the most from any specific outcome? Be flexible and allow your plans to change once you have assessed the situation.

Consider the following questions when trying to assess the cons: Is there some constraint (energy, knowledge, money, resources, space, or time) that will be violated? What are the requirements being placed on the problem? Who are imposing these requirements? Are there examples drawn from history or experience that have gone awry? Does the solution violate these requirements or constraints? Does this idea align with your strategy, values and goals? Does the proposal contradict the data that has been gathered? What contingency plans still need to be made? What consequence may arise from this solution? Will this solution be acceptable to the people involved? What could go wrong implementing this proposal? What are the potential pitfalls? What are the weaknesses that need to be addressed? What might go wrong if this idea is carried out? Does experience give any hints as to something that might go wrong? Does this solution align with the resources available? Are you lacking in connections, finances, knowledge, manpower, resources, skills, or tools? Do any facts indicate something might go wrong? What parts of the proposal are unfeasible, unusable, unworkable, or impractical? Is there anything about the solution that is illegal or immoral? What aspects of the proposal are inefficient? Will the idea be disruptive or too radical in any way? Are there aspects of the proposal that are unfair, unaesthetic or unappealing? Identify rational reasons for why a solution will not work, and you will have a springboard from which to engineer a solution that will work.

Next, focus on the pros. You need to develop a habit of finding merit. Learn to identify what is valuable in an idea. You may have one thousand good ideas, but it does no good if you can't see the value in any of them. Ideas have power and learning to recognize merit in them is the first step to harnessing that power. You can deliberately choose to find merit, value and benefit to an idea. That kind of choice is the hallmark of honing your thinking skills. Identifying merits is critical to turning potential ideas into kinetic power.

You might question what is the value in finding merit in an idea? If I just address the faults isn't that enough? What is the practical value of finding conceptual benefits? The truth is that better solutions are advanced by looking for the benefits. Entrepreneurs create entire industries by finding value in something that others dismissed. Genius is often finding value in an idea that others have overlooked. Fire thinking can also kindle new ideas. Looking for merit is a constructive and generative skill. Often concepts, proposals and suggestions will arise when searching for value. The reason for this is that the search for benefit entails looking for opportunity and improvements. Learn to explore and speculate when looking for merit in something.

Ask probing questions when identifying the merits of an idea. What are the benefits of this solution? What value does this idea have? When does it help? Who would find it worthwhile? Why is it an asset? What are you trying to solve? What do you hope to accomplish with the proposal? What results do you expect? Where specifically are you going with the idea? How does it help? Where does it have the most value? How does it generate value? What other merits are there? What reasons support the idea (evidence, experience, data, logical support, experiments, surveys, expert opinion, trends, and facts)? What are the possible benefits of this idea? What justifications can be given to support the proposal? What speculation, and hunches support this idea and why? What is the best possible scenario? What are the optimal benefits? What are extensions that can be made to the proposal? If the solution were implemented what would be the benefits? Under what conditions does the proposal become feasible? What are effective applications of the proposed idea? Will this get the job done? What alterations can be made to this idea so that it will get the job done? What other existing ideas can be employed in the current situation? Consider how well matched the proposal is to your resources? Is this the most effective solution? Why is this solution effective? How can this proposal be made more effective? By identifying the benefits of a proposal what new opportunities become available?

An expert has a lot of positive knowledge, but also a lot of negative knowledge. Thus, he knows the pitfalls and common mistakes that are commonly made. He has a lot of positive knowledge. That is, the knowledge needed for a plan to succeed. He can choose from a broad base of similar solutions that have effectively addressed similar problems. Judgment is a cornerstone of thinking (Hogarth, 1991). The techniques of Fire thinking will improve your skills of evaluation.

FIRE THINKING		
COMPONENT	DESCRIPTION	PRINCIPLES
Decision	Making tradeoffs and identifying selection criteria to make intelligent choices.	Goals & Objectives Constraints Alternatives Criteria Consequences Selection
Judgment	Arriving at objective, practical, wise, and reasonable conclusions & solutions through assessment and evaluation.	Experience Fallacies of Thinking Objectivity Scrutiny Wisdom
Contingency	Developing contingency plans by understanding risks and anticipating failure to adapt to changing circumstances	Vulnerability Hazard Response Contingency Plan
Validation	Ascertaining the truth of a matter by testing for reliability, and credibility of information.	Standards (Criterion of Truth) Consistency (Construct Validity) Prediction Reliability

Table 5 - Fire Thinking Components & Principles

Part II –Components & Principles of Elemental Thinking

Chapter 6 –Earth Thinking and Evidence

The first component among the elements of thinking is Evidence. Evidence is the available body of relevant facts and information which can be used to support a claim, belief, or proposition as valid or invalid. Evidence in the form of facts, information, observations, and knowledge form the basis of every action we take. Every decision we make, every plan that we execute, and everything we do is based on some evidence. The better your data, the more confident you can be of your results. To gather the relevant information for your thinking activities, you need to use the following principles. Use these principles to identify your assumptions, gather information, organize data and assess.

ASSUMPTIONS – When you are trying to analyze something or to think about anything, it is always useful to ask yourself what your assumptions are. Try to recognize knowledge that you may be taking for granted. Assumptions, bias, preconceived notions, prejudices, and information that you take as true without proof. Assumptions are vital to identify and acknowledge because they can skew the way you think. As we progress through life, and we come across enough instances of a notion we start taking that for granted, and we often label it common sense. Presuppositions can cloud your thinking and distort your view of reality.

When we hold an assumption, we take something for granted, we expect that something will be a specific way because it was that way in the past. We use assumptions constantly in our everyday lives. It is reasonable to make assumptions, but we should be aware of assumptions that hamper critical thinking. You should list the assumptions relevant to your problem. Until you do so, you may not even be aware of many of the assumptions you take for granted. Some assumptions will be evident as you work on a problem. Assumptions skew our view of a problem and its solution. A wrong assumption can steer you off course. Refer to your list of assumptions often. Question the validity of your assumptions. Ask if they are still appropriate. Assumptions cause you to take things for granted. If you assume something is true, you will not examine it critically. Assumptions hinder the refinement of your proposals. Try to minimize and identify your assumptions.

Be wary of the assumptions that others hold. Others who become familiar with your problem will settle into the same perspectives as you do. A typical assumption is that imperfections will be overlooked. Do not assume that if an idea is clear to you that it will be clear to others. Do not assume that people who stand to benefit most from your idea will accept it without any persuasion on your part.

Assumptions can be tricky to identify because they often hide in plain sight. Some fact which seems obvious might really be an assumption in disguise preying upon your mind. Explain the problem and solution to other people and pay attention to where they get confused. Listen to the questions they ask. That is a good way to ferret out your assumptions.

List your relevant assumptions. Write as many as you can think of. Keep a list. Add to the list as you work. Once you have identified assumptions, you can then work with them or around them. You can monitor your assumptions, you can address false assumptions, and you can avoid pitfalls opened by your assumptions.

GATHERING EVIDENCE – The start of any thinking journey begins with gathering evidence. You need to gather information pertinent to what you are investigating. Possible sources of information include: articles, the internet, journals, research papers, books, and experts of the subject. Gather and record information that you may find useful. Learn about the people, history, events, and available data on your chosen subject or problem of interest. Search articles, books, journals and research papers to find information that is pertinent to your problem. Ask yourself the journalistic questions of who, what, where, when, why and how. These may inspire and guide you your quest for information.

The gathering evidence principle of the evidence component requires diligence and industry. You can start with a search on your subject related to your problem. Next, seek out relevant blogs, videos, books, interviews, and articles. If there are any famous luminaries, or famous works that you recognize start with that. Explore each of these in turn. Take notes. Large projects will require sustained study over time. Pace yourself. Read, research, and study every day. Read the most relevant work first. Steady daily progress will build up your cache of evidence. Identify the most important ideas from a work. One source will point you to others.

A. DEPTH & BREADTH – If you dig deep enough you can find a tremendous amount of information on a subject. Breadth of knowledge is a basic understanding of a variety of things. Depth is the complexity of evidence. Breadth is the range and extent of evidence. Gathering a large quantity of information on a subject bestows perspective. Depth of evidence offers profound insights. Breadth of knowledge is useful when you want to survey a subject. Broad knowledge allows you to consider many avenues of thought. Breadth prompts you to explore in new directions which will further expand your base of evidence.

ORGANIZING INFORMATION – In any complex analysis you will have a large quantity of information that you need to process. Efficient analysis depends on your ability to access the relevant information. Gather and organize the information you have so that it is easy to access, grouped in a logical fashion, and useful to you. Some ways you may try to organize information are by: contacts, date, history, index, location, method, people, relationships, subject, time or topic.

While you are identifying assumptions and gathering a base of evidence you can start to organize your collected information. You should separate your collected data into concepts, facts, and opinions. This is an iterative and interactive process. As you get new information find a home for it. The following table summarizes factors to consider when organizing information:

Concepts	A concept is a general notion, or abstraction.
Facts	Body of information or propositions that are taken to be true.
Opinion	A viewpoint or belief held not necessarily based on fact or knowledge.
Observation	The use of your senses to register something as being significant with the objective of gaining information.
Source & Context	This pertains to source of gathered evidence, and the context by which information is obtained.

Table 6 - Earth thinking evidence: factors for organizing information

A. CONCEPTS – A concept is a general notion, or abstraction. A fact is an undisputable piece of information. An opinion is a viewpoint formed about something. Concepts can bring together information, observations, and perceptions.

One of the first things you need to do is to identify what are the most important concepts, themes, and abstractions that are important to the problem at hand.

B. FACTS –Facts are an available body of information or propositions that are taken to be true. In the validation component of Fire thinking this topic is explored extensively. Fact are reliable and credible. As you gather new information, you will encounter facts as information that is widely taken to be true by experts.

C. OPINION – An opinion is a viewpoint held by someone that is not necessarily based on fact. Categorize your available data into concepts, facts and opinions. We formulate opinions based on experience, evidence, testimony, observations, and circumstantial evidence. Opinions are the interplay between intuition and reasoning. Opinions can be important to making decisions and forming judgments.

D. OBSERVATION – What personal experiences can you draw from? What observations can you use from other people's experiences? Observations are made from your senses typically produce the most reliable evidence. Use your sight, sounds, tastes, touch, and smell to explore the situation at hand. Sights are captured in graphics, videos, and photographs. Sounds are captured in recordings.

E. SOURCE & CONTEXT – Consider the source of information and the context from which that evidence was generated. Who formulated the theory, performed the experiment, made the assertion, or wrote the paper? Where was the data gathered and how? When was the data gathered? What were the circumstances, environment, and context? Did the scene or setting influence the information? Did the situation, political climate, or current affairs have an influence?

ASSESSMENT – Once you have considered your assumptions, gathered your facts, and organized your facts. You need to assess them. You can apply the validation component of Fire thinking now. Consider the accuracy, interpretation, relevance, reliability, subjectivity, objectivity, and universals from your gathered information. These are some factors to consider when assessing information:

Accuracy and precision	The quality and exactness of a measurement, calculation or specification.
Interpretation and Inference	Inference makes conclusions from evidence and reasoning rather than explicit statements. Interpretation explains the meaning and significance.
Relevance	Information which is pertinent or germane to the matter at hand.
Reliability	This is the consistency of measurement. Investigation that produces similar evidence under consistent conditions.
Subjective vs	Subjective is being influenced by personal feelings

Objective	and opinions. Objective is to be free of personal feelings and opinions.
Universal & Particular	Universal statements make a claim about an entire class of things. Particular statements make an assertion about a specific thing.

Table 7 - Earth thinking evidence: assessing information factors

A. ACCURACY & PRECISION – The accuracy and precision of your measurements, and information is important to consider. If there is a calculation or computation involved, the precision and method of calculation can be analyzed. You can consider how the information was obtained, and the quality of the data. Questionable information can be a cue for further investigation.

B. INTERPRETATION & INFERENCE - Consider what conclusions have already been drawn, and what can you infer from those conclusions. Inference makes a conclusion from evidence and reasoning rather than from explicit statements. Interpretation is the act of explaining the meaning and significance of something. Try to identify what interpretations have been made. Considering all your available information, what inferences can you draw?

C. RELEVANCE – Relevance of information is defined as data which is pertinent or germane to the matter at hand. Of all the possible facts that you might come across, only certain information will be important to your situation. When the situation changes, different information may become relevant. Information which can be applied or associated in your situation is relevant.

D. RELIABILITY OF FACTS - Reliability is the consistency of a measurement. Reliability pertains to investigation that produces similar evidence under consistent conditions. Reliability is a principle of the validity component of Fire thinking. It establishes the truth. Ontological truth deals with the existence of something. Logical truth deals with the validity of statements. Establishing the truth is a matter of determining if something has a basis in fact. Science tries to determine the truths about our universe. Be wary of statements that contradict each other. An argument with contradictory premises denies conclusions being drawn from them.

E. SUBJECTIVE VERSUS OBJECTIVE - Distinguish objective versus subjective aspects of your body of evidence. Separate fact from opinion. Build upon the objective facts. Express your subjective opinion. Arriving at the truth requires reconciling subjective experiences with objective facts. The truth is independent of emotion and belief by the masses. The truth cannot be established by pity, prestige, force, ridicule, or ignorance. Be wary of opinions presented as facts. Cherry-picked facts, supporting a predetermined conclusion are suspect.

F. UNIVERSALS & PARTICULARS– Be cognizant of universal statements. The words "all", "some", and "every" signify universal statements. Universal statements make claims about a class of things. Particular statements make assertions about a specific thing. Make statements as precise as your knowledge permits. "All" and "every" imply 100% of the time. If you mean 75-99% of the time, use "most". If you mean 50% use "half" of the time. If know an exact percentage then state that. What holds true for a collective may not be true for each component. What holds true for a member may not pertain to the entire class. Universal statements may not apply to special cases. Universal statements crafted from sparse samples is hasty generalization. *Hasty generalizations* are often biased. Establish a universal generalization only by obtaining a representative number of samples, not by simple enumeration of instances.

EARTH THINKING – EVIDENCE		
COMPONENT	**PRINCIPLE**	**DESCRIPTION**
	Assumptions	Something that is accepted to be true or certain to happen without proof.
	Gathering Evidence	Search in the internet, articles, journals, research papers, and books. Learn about the people, history, events, and available data.
EVIDENCE	Organizing Information	Organizing facts relevant to your situation or problem. Store, sort, and index information for easy access.
	Assessment	Consider the accuracy and precision, interpretation and inference, relevance, reliability, subjectivity, objectivity, universals, and particulars of your gathered information.

Table 8 - Earth thinking evidence component principles

Chapter 7 –Earth Thinking and Deductive Reasoning

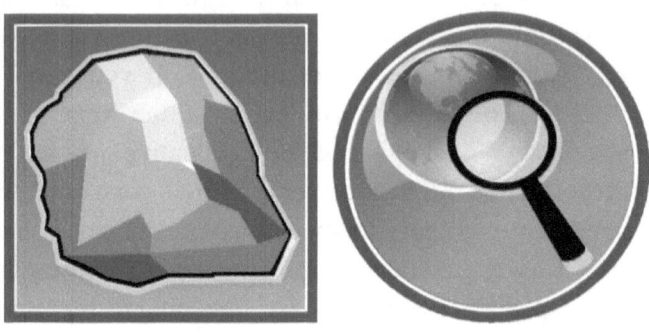

Deductive reasoning arrives at specific conclusions from general principles. The use of universal premises, theory, or rules allows a thinker to forward a hypothesis (Terrell, 1967). Then, he draws a conclusion based on reasoning, analysis and evidence.

Deduction is often used in logical arguments. Deductive arguments assert that the conclusion necessarily follows from the truth of the premises. Deduction follows four main steps: A theory, hypothesis, evidence, and confirmation (Terrell, 1967). A theory is a system of ideas that is intended to explain something, often based on general principles. From these general principles, a hypothesis is proposed as a given explanation for something. Evidence is then gathered that is related to the hypothesis. Lastly, confirmation for or against the hypothesis can be determined by analyzing the evidence.

STEPS IN DEDUCTION	
STEP	**DESCRIPTION**
THEORY	A theory is a system of ideas intended to explain something usually based on general principles. A theory may also be a set of principles on which the practice of an activity is based (for example a theory of political practice). At a personal level, it might be an idea that is used to account for a situation or justify a course of action (for example a theory of why your friend feels happy).

HYPOTHESIS	A hypothesis is a proposed explanation made based on limited evidence as a starting point for further investigation. A hypothesis is proposed as a basis for reasoning without any presumptions as to its truthfulness. A hypothesis should account for *assumptions*.
EVIDENCE	Observations and facts are gathered related to the hypothesis. See the Evidence component of Earth thinking for more details.
CONFIRMATION	The evidence is analyzed to determine whether conclusions can be drawn. Typically, the objective is to ascertain if the hypothesis can be supported or denied. It may also suggest if further investigation is necessary. An argument, syllogism, critical reasoning, and formal logic can be applied to assist in determining whether a hypothesis is true or false.

Table 9 - Earth thinking: Steps in deduction

THEORY – A theory is a system of ideas used to explain something based on general principles. An economic theory would be used to explain the production and consumption of goods and services in relationship to the wealth and resources of a country or region. A theory may also be a set of principles upon which the practice of an activity is based. A theory of medical practice is based upon human biological sciences and a history of medical outcomes. Closer to home, at a personal level, a theory might be an idea that you used to account for a situation or justify a course of action. Theories form the basis of deductive reasoning. Deductions reason from general principles to specific conclusions.

HYPOTHESIS – A hypothesis is a supposition or explanation proposed based on limited evidence as a starting point for further investigation. Inductive reasoning requires you to take specific facts and specific instances and proceed to generalizations and generalized rules. The process of inductive reasoning then involves making a hypothesis. You need to make an educated guess to produce a generalization or general rule. Human insight and intuition supported by a body of evidence allows us to offer a supposition. When making a hypothesis you may find it helpful to use Water thinking to find linkages between disparate pieces of evidence. Finding these links will help you craft a generalization. Two of the key components of Water thinking: linking and synthesis can help you generate a hypothesis. There will be situations where Air thinking will also be useful.

Creativity and unconventional thinking may be just the leap of insight that is needed to formulate a hypothesis.

ASSUMPTION – An assumption is something taken to be true or certain to happen without proof. Assumptions need to be accounted for during hypothesis formulation. Because assumptions are taken for granted to be true, they can lead to faulty conclusions if they turn out to be false. Furthermore, it is important to list your key assumptions so that you are aware of what you are taking for gratis. Assumptions in the form of bias and preconceptions can cloud your judgment and thinking. Assumptions can also be useful because they allow people to build new notions and ideas without having to reinvent their understanding of the world.

ARGUMENT – An argument is a reason or set of reasons given with the aim of persuading others that an action or idea is right or wrong. *Arguments are used in the confirmation step of deduction.* Arguments illustrate your line of reasoning. A conclusion can be supported through evidence, deduction. A syllogism-type argument is composed of two basic elements: premises and a conclusion. Sound reasoning is founded upon reliable evidence and logic. Investigation depends on reliable evidence. Reliability relates to the truth of the information.

There are four steps to developing a deductive argument:

1. **STATE ARGUMENT** – The first step is to develop an argument, a line of reasoning. You will gather and organize your evidence. Then you need to identify your assumptions. State what you know about your problem in the form of premises. You need to identify any hidden premises. What are your objectives and what do you know? What are your unknowns and is there a problem you are trying to solve? Organize your thoughts and try to develop a line of reasoning that will take you from your assumptions and premises to a conclusion.

2. **EXAMINE ARGUMENT** – The second step is to examine each part of the argument for errors. Make sure that the argument is relevant to the problem. You will gain insight by playing devil's advocate and challenging the argument. Challenge the assumptions and ask questions that probe the issue.

3. **VALIDATE REASONING** – The third step is to examine the line of reasoning for validity errors. The objective is to identify flaws in reasoning. The

reasoning used to travel from the premise to the conclusion should be thoroughly considered. You can then determine if the conclusion is legitimate.

4. **REVISE ARGUMENT** – The last step is to revise your argument. You should refine your reasoning and purge it of logical errors. Sometimes only minor changes are needed, perhaps adding a qualification. Occasionally, the change required is dramatic. You may need to abandon the solution and start again. Updates may be spurred by new evidence, a new line of reasoning, altered objectives, a change of plan, or flaws in reasoning that you have identified.

PREMISE – A premise is a previous statement or proposition from which another is inferred as a conclusion. The validity of a premise is crucial in the development of a sound argument. Invalid premises can lead to false conclusions even if the line of reasoning is logical. A premise is akin to an assumption because it is used as a foundation for further deductive work. *Premises need to be accounted for in the evidence and confirmation steps of deductive reasoning.*

Good reasoning depends on sound evidence and reasoning. The evidence is sound if you have built your solution from reliable and valid data. Facts, instead of opinion, should form the basis of your reasoning. Sound reasoning is the process used to get to your conclusions. The premises need to be true and relevant.

CONFIRMATION & CONCLUSION – A conclusion is a judgment or decision reached through reasoning. Conclusions are the end of a journey but serve as the springboard for action.

The confirmation of a hypothesis allows you to draw a conclusion based on your available evidence. A solution to a problem is also type of conclusion. A conclusion is the result of reasoning which might be deliberate or unpremeditated. When you apply reasoning, you gather your premises, work through the logical steps, create hypotheses, gather evidence, test the hypotheses, confirm or deny the hypothesis, refine your viewpoint, and finally arrive at a conclusion.

When developing a line of reasoning in the confirmation step of deductive reasoning, you want to see if the experiments and evidence support a hypothesis. You are trying to draw a specific conclusion or interpretation of a general principle from the available evidence. Careful evaluation will allow you to analyze the argument and identify the premises, hypothesis, assumptions, and conclusion.

In conclusion, remember that deduction involves starting from the general and proceeds to the particular (Terrell, 1967). Induction works in an opposite fashion, by starting with the particular and proceeding to a universal. Both deduction and induction possess two elements common to all logical arguments - a premise and a conclusion. Deduction breaks down a general truth into its constituent parts. You start with universal rules, principles, or scientific law relevant to your problem. From general laws, you can identify specific situations that you can apply rules to. You develop a hypothesis that might explain a situation, gather evidence, and try to confirm or deny the hypothesis based on that evidence.

EARTH THINKING – DEDUCTIVE REASONING		
EARTH COMPONENT	PRINCIPLE	DESCRIPTION
DEDUCTIVE REASONING	Formal Logic	Formal logic is based on arguments involving deductive reasoning using relationships and including the use of syllogisms and mathematical symbols.
	Assumption	An assumption is something taken to be true or certain to happen without proof.
	Argument	An argument is a reason or set of reasons given with the aim of persuading others that an action or idea is right or wrong.
	Syllogism	A syllogism is a form of reasoning whereby a conclusion is drawn from two given or assumed propositions (premises). The conclusion may be valid or invalid. Each of which the premises share a term with the conclusion and shares a common or middle term not present in the conclusion.
	Premise	A premise is a previous statement or proposition from which another is inferred as a conclusion.
	Conclusion	A conclusion is a judgment or decision reached through reasoning.

Table 10 - Earth thinking Deductive reasoning component principles

Chapter 8 –Earth Thinking and Inductive Reasoning

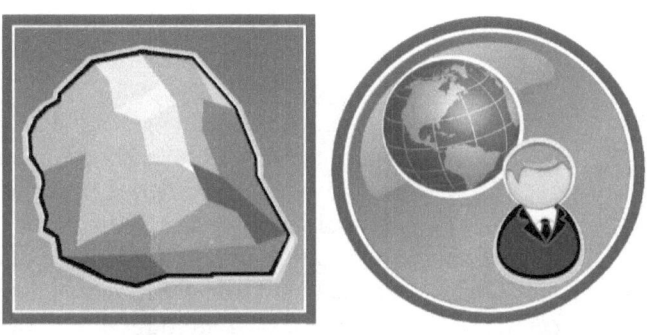

Induction involves starting from the particular and proceeds to the general. Induction produces probable conclusions given a set of particulars. Both deduction and induction possess two elements common to all logical arguments - a premise and a conclusion. Induction puts the particular facts together to serve as a body of evidence which provide the basis for making a reliable generalization. A hypothesis is formed from observation, or calculated reasoning. Science employs inductive reasoning. Scientists gather data and discern patterns from the data. Once a pattern is detected, reliable predictions and generalizations can be made (Copi, Cohen, & Flage, 2007).

The basic steps of induction are: pattern, hypothesis, experiment, and theory (Copi, Cohen, & Flage, 2007). The first thing to do is to gather what you know about the topic of interest. Gathering evidence is one of the main components of Earth thinking. Then, you find important associations in the data. Water thinking will help you find associations. A hypothesis is proposed which may explain and account for the pattern of evidence. Finally, a general theory, rule or conclusion is developed based on the evidence and hypothesis.

STEPS IN INDUCTION	
STEP	**DESCRIPTION**
PATTERN	Relationships are identified among the data. Water thinking can be used to identify patterns within your body of evidence.
HYPOTHESIS	A hypothesis is a proposed explanation made based on limited evidence as a starting point for further investigation. A hypothesis is proposed as a basis for

	reasoning without any presumptions as to its truthfulness. A hypothesis should account for assumptions.
EXPERIMENT	Experiments are a scientific procedure undertaken to make a discovery, test a hypothesis, or demonstrate a known fact. Experiments are often performed to gather evidence supporting or denying the hypothesis.
THEORY	A theory is a system of ideas intended to explain something usually based on general principles. A theory may also be a set of principles on which the practice of an activity is based. At a personal level, it might be an idea that is used to account for a situation or justify a course of action. The evidence is analyzed to determine whether conclusions can be drawn. The objective in inductive reasoning is to ascertain if the hypothesis can be supported or denied. It may also suggest further investigation is necessary. Critical reasoning, and formal logic can be applied to assist in determining whether a hypothesis is true or false.

Table 11 - Earth thinking: Steps in Induction

GENERALIZATION – A generalization is the expansion of a concept with less specific criteria. Generalizations are one of the foundational elements of logic and reasoning. Generalizations are essential to inferences. Generalizations seek common characteristics shared by a set of elements. They are the basis of all valid deductive inferences. As with all claims, generalizations need to be validated as changing circumstances may alter the nature of the shared characteristics. A formal definition of generalization is: if every instance of concept A can be subsumed within concept B. Then, B can be said to be a generalization of A. The reverse concept is a specialization, particularization, or a special case. If there are instances of concept A which are not instances of concept B.

HYPOTHESIS – A hypothesis is a supposition or explanation proposed based on limited evidence as a starting point for further investigation. Inductive reasoning requires you to take particular facts and specific instances and proceed to generalizations and generalized rules. The process of inductive reasoning then involves making a hypothesis. You need to make an educated guess to produce a generalization or general rule. Human insight and intuition supported by a body of evidence allows us to create a supposition.

Hypotheses are used in science to propose an explanation for a natural phenomenon. Scientists base new hypotheses on observations they have made on natural phenomena. The hypotheses will undergo scrutiny, verification and testing. Once the scientific method has been employed, extensive testing is performed, and the hypothesis becomes generally accepted as the accurate explanation for the phenomena, the scientific hypothesis will become a scientific theory.

EXPERIMENT – An experiment is a procedure with the aim of verifying, refuting, or establishing a hypothesis. We often associate experimentation with scientific discoveries, and scientific theories because that is one of its major uses. Experiments are performed by lab scientists in white coats in a research laboratory. However, they can also be performed by anyone. Experimentation is employed to verify a hypothesis or verify a claim. Experimentation can be used to test a claim. It might be something as simple as a conversation with someone. It does not necessarily have to involve white lab coats and chemistry beakers. The objective of scientific experimentation is to find out if a hypothesis is true.

An experiment can also be a detailed investigation or a test of the performance, qualities, or suitability of something. Experimentation can be used a tool for mental exploration and discovery. Use experimentation with the aim of gaining insight and knowledge. Suppose you have a hypothesis that you will enjoy sky diving. Without jumping out of a plane, how could you first test that hypothesis? You might try experiment with a simulator or conduct an experiment with a virtual reality computer program.

SCIENTIFIC METHOD – The scientific method has been the basis of our understanding of the universe around us. The method involves systematic observation, measurement, and experimentation. It is based upon the formulation, testing, and modification of a hypothesis to explain natural phenomenon. Scientific understanding starts with a hypothesis. A scientific hypothesis proposes an idea to explain a phenomenon. These ideas are tested through observation and experimentation. The experimentation affirms or denies the hypothesis. We build on those ideas that are promising and reject those that are not. Scientists and thinkers follow the evidence wherever it leads them. They establish scientific theories from consistent results from repeated experimentation and observation. They continue to question everything to develop further insight and formulate more refined hypotheses. Eventually, mathematic models and equations can be used to predict how things will behave in nature.

The scientific method consists of five parts: the formulation of a question, the development of a hypothesis, prediction, testing, and analysis. The start of many thinking endeavors begins with a good question. The hypothesis is then used to formulate a conjecture to explain the observations and evidence. Scientific formulations define a null hypothesis which is the conjecture that the statistical hypothesis is false while an alternative hypothesis exhibits the desired outcome. A prediction determines the logical consequences of a hypothesis. If the hypothesis aligns with observation and evidence, and can explain a phenomenon, it should have predictive value. Scientific experiments are designed to test and verify a hypothesis. After experiments are performed and data is gathered, analysis is used to ascertain the validity of the hypothesis. Statistical analysis is typically used. An ANOVA, t-test, or chi-squared test are used to mathematically estimate a confidence level of the hypothesis.

STEPS IN SCIENTIFIC METHOD	
STEP	**DESCRIPTION**
FORMULATION OF QUESTION	Developing a question will serve as the basis for a scientific study. Questions will guide the thinking journey and serve as the basis for exploring the unknown.
DEVELOPMENT OF HYPOTHESIS	A hypothesis is a proposed explanation made based on limited evidence as a starting point for further investigation. A hypothesis is proposed as a basis for reasoning without any presumptions as to its truthfulness. A hypothesis should account for assumptions. Scientific formulations define a null hypothesis which is the conjecture that the statistical hypothesis is false while an alternative hypothesis exhibits the desired outcome.
PREDICTION	A prediction determines the logical consequences of a hypothesis. If the hypothesis aligns observations and available evidence to explain a phenomenon, it should have predictive value.
TESTING	Scientific experiments are designed to test and verify a hypothesis.
ANALYSIS	After experiments are performed and data is gathered, analysis is used to ascertain the validity of the hypothesis.

Table 12 - Earth thinking: Steps in the Scientific Method

THEORY & CONCLUSION – Conclusions are the product of inductive reasoning. Statistical analysis performed on the experimental data produce conclusions related to the hypothesis. Fundamentally, a conclusion is a judgment or decision reached by reasoning. A conclusion is generally formed from a carefully thought out line of reasoning, experimentation, observation, and analysis.

Conclusions are not necessarily true. However, the most useful ones to us we hold to be true. But even conclusions that determine that a hypothesis is false can have value. We value scientific discoveries and scientific theories because scientists dedicate their lives to asking questions, proposing hypothesis, executing experiments, and generating conclusions. Conclusions are reached by evidence and the logic of the arguments.

EARTH THINKING – INDUCTIVE REASONING		
EARTH COMPONENT	**PRINCIPLE**	**DESCRIPTION**
INDUCTIVE REASONING	Generalization	A generalization is the expansion of a concept with less specific criteria. Generalizations are one of the foundational elements of logic and reasoning. Generalizations are essential to inferences.
	Hypothesis	A hypothesis is a supposition or explanation proposed based on limited evidence as a starting point for further investigation.
	Experiment	An experiment is a procedure with the aim of verifying, refuting, or establishing a hypothesis. An experiment can also be a detailed investigation or a test of the performance, qualities, or suitability of something.
	Scientific Method	The scientific method is a procedure that has characterized the study of the sciences since the 17th century. The method consists in systematic observation, measurement, and experiment, and the formulation, testing, and modification of hypotheses.
	Conclusion	A conclusion is a judgment or decision reached by reasoning.

Table 13 - Earth thinking Inductive reasoning component principles

Chapter 9 –Earth Thinking and Abductive Reasoning

Abductive reasoning was first introduced by Charles Sanders Peirce, an American philosopher. This is a form of logical inference is focused on arriving at a reasonable conclusion through the available evidence (Peirce, 1992). In abductive reasoning, unlike deductive reasoning, the premises do not guarantee a conclusion. This type of reasoning is used in the disciplines of law, computer science, diagnosticians, detectives, artificial intelligence, and scientific research.

As with deductive and inductive reasoning the evidence component plays a key role in abductive reasoning. Start with the principles from the evidence component of Earth thinking: *assumptions*, *gathering evidence*, *organizing information*, and *assessment*. Gathering and managing relevant evidence inaugurates any journey of thinking.

CAUSALITY – Everything that physically exists and everything that happens in the universe has some cause. Something is the cause of another because either it explains the existence of that thing, or it explains some aspect of that thing, called a *"mode of its existence"* (McInerny, 2005). Humans innately desire to know why things happen. We are curious about what causes any natural phenomena. To know the cause of something, is to know that thing profoundly. In more practical terms, knowing the cause allows you to modify and understand the effect.

Aristotle proposed that there are four types of causes: "efficient cause", "material cause", "formal cause", and "final causes". An efficient cause is one which creates or modifies something. An efficient cause is perhaps the most basic cause of something (Aristotle, The Organon: The Works of Aristotle on Logic, 2012). A final cause is the purpose of an activity. A material cause is the substance that an object is composed of. The formal cause is a thing that precisely identifies the nature of something. Francis Bacon wrote in his *Advancement of Learning*, material and efficient causes are the ones which are relevant modern science (Bacon & Kitchin, 2000).

Understanding causes and effects can play a vital role in reasoning because it allows you to determine what should logically follow based on your collected evidence. By observing effects, and finding their motive cause, you can gain a better understanding of any problem. When you observe some effect, develop the habit of rationalizing its cause and make a mental note of it. This skill is important to efficient reasoning. Finally, keep in mind that some effects can have multiple causes. The world is a complex place. We would like to believe that the world's problems all have one root cause, that our problems all have one silver bullet. Instead, usually the interplay of compound causes shapes outcomes.

SIMPLICITY – Simplify your solution without sacrificing functionality. Brevity leads to clarity. Simplicity leads to elegance. Clear and elegant solutions are the mark of genius. Precision dispels confusion. Non-sequiturs lead to complexity. Non-sequiturs are extraneous elements in a line of reasoning.

Consider the following questions to strive for simplicity: Is there any part of the solution that can be removed? Does each part of the solution have a purpose? Can two parts be merged without losing any functionality? Is there anything that does not belong? How could the solution be simplified? How could the solution be restructured to make it simpler yet equally effective? Can the problem be broken down into more manageable parts? Economy of thought is a mark of proficient and methodical thinking. Seeking the simplest explanations for something as inspired by Occam's razor is part and parcel of abductive reasoning.

DECOMPOSITION – Break down a complicated problem, system, or concept into pieces. Once you have broken down the problem you can work with each component. This will make the system more manageable and tractable. You can also divide your solution into modules. You might consider breaking your solution down in time as well as space. A series of steps in time is a procedure.

There are many ways that a problem or a solution can be modularized. You can break down the problem based on any combination of: concepts, deliverables, finance, form, function, location, resources, space, or time.

Decomposition facilitates abductive reasoning as it makes thinking about the logical steps easier. Small pieces are more manageable and easier to consider than the entire system. Abductive reasoning may also employ deductive or inductive reasoning. Making logical connections, using Water thinking, and wrapping your mind around an issue are all facilitated through decomposition. The linking and synthesis components of Water thinking are also aimed at helping you think about decomposing a complex problem into more manageable elements.

OCCAM'S RAZOR – William of Ockham (1287 – 1347) formulated a problem-solving method based on a principle of parsimony, economy, and succinctness. He wrote, "plurality must never be posited without necessity." This is translated from the Latin phrase *"Numquam ponendo est pluritas sine necessitate."* The principle of Occam's Razor is the assertion is that among competing hypotheses, the one with the fewest assumptions should be selected. Complicated solutions may eventually prove correct. But, in the absence of evidence, the fewer assumptions that are employed the better. As a heuristic, scientists employ Occam's Razor to sharpen theoretical models. It is used with the scientific method based on the criteria of falsification, trying to prove a theory to be false. Phenomena have numerous possible causes. In the battle of explanations, the simpler theories win out over complex ones because they are better testable and falsifiable. Occam's Razor has made an appearance in many branches of science and philosophy. The "razor" part of Occam's Razor refers to distinguishing between two hypotheses either by "shaving away" unnecessary assumptions or cutting apart two similar conclusions (Sober, 2015).

In his work, *Posterior Analytics*, Aristotle wrote, "we may assume the superiority *ceteris paribus* [all things being equal] of the demonstration which derives from fewer postulates or hypotheses. (Aristotle, Posterior Analytics, 350 BCE)" Ptolemy (c. AD 90 – c. AD 168) stated, "We consider it a good principle to explain the phenomena by the simplest hypothesis possible. (Franklin, 2002)" Knowledge secured from inquiry with no premises outclasses that with few assumptions. The fewer assumptions made the better. In 1960, Ray Solomonoff gave a mathematical formulation of Occam's Razor in his theory of universal inductive inference, a theory of prediction based on observations (Rathmanner & Hutter, 2011). Occam's Razor has empirical, practical, and aesthetic appeal. A simple hypothesis to explain something is mentally attractive. Simple models may capture underlying structure better than complex ones, and thus may have better predictive performance, are easier to understand, and not as involved to verify. If two theories explain the data equally well, the simpler theory is going to be more amenable to testing and verification. Its empirical content is greater (Sober, 2015).

HOW? AND WHY? – Two of the most powerful questions you can ask are "How?" and "Why?" They are valuable tools in your thinker's toolkit. Use them to continually probe and deepen your analysis. Ask and seek answers to these two powerful questions.

At the heart of the "why?" question is curiosity. The question is probing for a deeper understanding of the nature of something. Posing the question prompts you to think about causes and effects, the entire system, compositions and decompositions, root causes and symptoms, explanations and hypothesis. The question "why?" is a powerful tool in your mental toolbox because can lead you down an avenue of inquiry that you might have otherwise overlooked. Also, the question gets people to consider their motivations, aspirations, and desires.

The purpose of "how?" is to get you to think about the mechanics of something. This question will make you think about the functional aspects of a system, the operation of a machine, and the steps in a process. The question "how?" is useful because it urges you to consider what makes a thing work. How the parts of a system interact together is at the heart of this question.

CONCLUSION – Conclusions are the end-product of abductive reasoning. The problem is stated, evidence is gathered, questions are posed, the system is decomposed, explanations are offered, and hypotheses are verified. Fundamentally, a conclusion is a judgment or decision reached by reasoning. A conclusion is generally formed from a carefully thought out line of reasoning, experimentation, observation, data gathering, and analysis. A conclusion from abductive reasoning should be a reasonable conclusion that fits the available evidence. We value the process of detective work because they methodically ask probing questions, gather meaningful evidence, propose insightful hypothesis, and arrive at sensible conclusions. Conclusions are reached by careful consideration of the available evidence, the system, the context, the people, and the processes.

EARTH THINKING – ABDUCTIVE REASONING		
EARTH	PRINCIPLE	DESCRIPTION

COMPONENT		
ABDUCTIVE REASONING	Causality	A relationship between two events, where the first event (the cause) induces the second event (the effect) to occur. It is a set of factors (cause) and their relationship to their phenomena (effect). The connection between a cause and an effect is also called a causal nexus.
	Occam's Razor	Named after William of Ockham (1287 – 1347), Occam's Razor is a principle of economy and succinctness in problem-solving stating that among competing hypotheses, the one with the fewest assumptions should be selected. More complicated solutions may prove correct, however, in the absence of evidence, the fewer assumptions that are employed the better.
	Decomposition	Decomposition during reasoning is the act of breaking down a problem into more manageable parts for easier analysis. Decomposition also assists in organizing concepts and promotes methodical analysis.
	Simplicity	Simplicity is expressed during reasoning with economy of thought, Occam's razor, minimal solutions, essential evidence, and identifying key pivots.
	How? & Why?	Two of the most useful questions in the thinker's toolkit. Ask "how?" and "why?" frequently to probe and deepen your analysis.
	Conclusion	A conclusion is a judgment or decision reached by reasoning.

Table 14 - Earth thinking Abductive reasoning component principles

Chapter 10 – Air Thinking and Investigation

Investigation is comprised of the principles of curiosity, examination, experimentation, exploration, and inquiry. It complements the evidence component of Earth thinking but with an eye towards creativity. Curiosity encourages you to ask probing questions, seek out the unknown, and study your subject matter thoroughly. Examination fosters creativity through your powers of observation. Experimentation seeks to develop hands on experiences to broaden your investigations. Experiments are used to broaden your horizons, open new avenues of exploration. Exploration encourages you to explore your terra incognita. Inquiry formulates questions to stimulate creativity.

CURIOSITY - there are several things you can do to stimulate your curiosity. Curiosity and formulating good questions will stimulate your creativity.

A. **ALTERNATIVES** – Searching for alternatives stimulates creativity by counteracting natural tendencies. The inclination of the mind is to settle down on one view. There is comfort in certainty, existing patterns, and old habits. Deliberately looking for alternate solutions will create possibilities. When you set out to look for alternatives, you will often find them. Ask yourself what other possibilities exist? What alternatives are there? What are other solutions?

B. **ASK QUESTIONS** –Questions assist in decisions, direct your goals, explore options, find connections, focus your investigation, generate ideas, inspire your creativity, shape your thinking, and sharpen your insight. Learn to ask probing questions. Consider the following questions: Why is this interesting? How can a new idea be generated? Where does this idea lead? What new hypothesis can be made? Is there a feasible variation? Can you modify a goal? Are there options? What preconceptions are there? What are the roadblocks? Are there existing solutions? Can the problem be decomposed? Can existing solutions be improved? Are you solving the wrong problem? What options exist?

C. **BE OBSERVANT** – Look at things carefully. Listen to people attentively. Observe how things work. Focus on the details to train your powers of observation. Note the speech patterns, mannerisms, dress, and dialogue when you interact with people. Being observant is an important aspect of being curious because it helps you spot things to investigate. Being curious, in turn, stimulates creativity. Creativity coaxes you to explore new possibilities and stay mentally active.

D. **BREAK BAD HABITS** – To instill curiosity and nurture creativity, you must break bad thinking habits. You need to become aware of your bad mental habits. Humans are creatures of habit. You can break your conditioning by interrupting your habitual thinking pattern. Identify a good habit to replace the old habit.

E. **ESCAPE PATTERNS** – To stimulate creativity, you must escape familiar ways of interpreting experiences. You need to break free of conformity, limiting beliefs, preconceived notions, prejudices, self-deception, and stereotypes which limit your curiosity and creativity. Consider absurd ideas to provoke your thinking. Identify what you take for granted about a situation and then deliberately break that pattern. Take any concept, idea, or word and use it to generate solutions.

F. **FIND OPPORTUNITY IN CONTROVERSY** – Exploit the real gem in controversy. There is an opportunity to explore new perspectives, enrich your understanding, and be mentally adventurous. A controversial issue is a matter that informed people disagree upon. Intelligent thinkers disagree based on competing values, disputable facts, different interpretations, and rational conclusions. Usually, there is some validity to both sides of a controversy.

G. **INTERESTING ASPECTS** – List all the interesting aspects of your subject. Why is this unusual aspect interesting? Consider variations to make a solution. Become immersed in the subject. Innovation often stems from persistence. The more you feed your mind, the greater the creativity reservoir. This gives you chance to make creative strides. It gets you look from different points of view.

H. **LINES OF THOUGHT** – The more open lines of thought you can keep on a subject, the more you will expand your thinking. People desire to make sense of things which may cause you to lock into a specific viewpoint. Healthy curiosity and intellectual honesty require you to consider arguments that threaten your viewpoint. Good thinkers ask the questions that poor thinkers ignore.

I. **ROOT CAUSES** – People who invent, make breakthroughs, and attain insights take time to wonder. They consider the root causes of things. They think about how things got to be the way they are, and what causes things to happen. The key to searching for causes is to be attuned to things that you cannot explain. Practice this when you come across news. What might have been the cause?

J. **PINPOINT IMPERFECTIONS** – Look for imperfections in things. This motivates creativity because you will identify where improvements can be made. Productive thinkers have a good sense of imperfection. They realize that all concepts, ideas, inventions, processes, systems, and tools are open to improvement. Creativity occurs by making a solution that overcomes a flaw.

K. **IMPLICATIONS** – Like a stone cast into a still pond, ideas have a wake that ripples outward. Good thinkers are sensitive to the implication of an idea. They recognize the potential impact of an idea before others do. Ask yourself what things this idea could impact? What will be influenced because of this new concept? What are the likely consequences? When would these events unfold?

L. **DISSATISFACTIONS** – Observe when people are dissatisfied. Take note of when you are dissatisfied with something. Experiences of anxiety, dissatisfaction, are opportunities in disguise. Viewed from a neutral observer's perspective, every dissatisfaction is some need that is not being met. Every nuisance is an open invitation for ingenuity. Creativity arises when people ponder how a dissatisfying situation can be improved. Dissatisfaction is the mother of invention.

M. **EXPERIMENTATION** – Vera and Crossan studied how the skills of improvisation performers can stimulate creativity (Vera & Crossan, 2005). They identified practice; collaboration; agree, accept, add; be present in the moment; and draw on reincorporation and ready-mades as the five key skills of improvisation. The practice of agree, accept, and add develops an experimental culture. The actors accept, support, and enhance ideas expressed by other improvisors. An experimental attitude will promote creativity. Try new things, be open-minded, accept diverse viewpoints, experiment, and entertain different perspectives.

EXAMINATION – Examination is a detailed inspection or investigation of a subject, concept, idea, proposal or problem. The objective is to scrutinize and inspect something. This principle of Air thinking performs a thorough investigation of your subject matter. You can examine something with all your senses. You can perform an examination using all the tools that you have available. You can examine the history, the physical make-up, composition, and available data on the topic of interest.

EXPERIMENTATION – Experimentation is the act of conducting a test under controlled conditions to demonstrate a known truth or to determine the efficacy of an idea. Experimentation requires the willingness to try new things and explore new ways of thinking. Experiments can come in many forms, some simple and others elaborate. The idea of experimentation is to get at the truth through a test that is designed to verify an assertion. When you design a test, you want to consider the variables, environment, unknowns, subjects, available evidence, and time constraints. Trochim described three kinds of studies: descriptive, relational and causal (Trochim, 2001). Descriptive tests are used to describe a situation or describe something. Relational tests try to establish a connection between two or more variables. Causal experiments are aimed at establishing a cause and effect patterns between variables. When you design a test, you need to consider variables, validity, problem formulation, data sampling, measurement, data reliability, surveys, questionnaires, interviews, scaling, and observation.

Experimentation begins with asking the questions and formulating a possible answer to that question, the hypothesis. You can try to verify its validity through an experiment. Curiosity creates new avenues for inquiry.

Experimentation is a willingness to try something new. Experiments are a good way to explore a subject or concept. Personal preferences or dislikes can be established through experiments. Scientists use experiments to formally establish causal relationships. Experiments can be used to validate a hypothesis or help to establish the truth of an assertion.

EXPLORATION – Exploration is an analysis of an idea, concept, proposal, subject or theme that is usually unfamiliar to learn more about it. The objective is to investigate. How can exploration further investigation? Investigation can be fostered with the methodical questioning of inquiry, the patient practice of experimentation, and careful observations through examination. Exploration nudges you to deliberately seek the unknown. What avenues of inquiry have not yet been pursued? What has not yet been tried with your experiments? What other things are waiting to be asked? What experts can you seek for advice? Where can you visit to broaden your experience related to your chosen topic of study? What relevant historical points need to be sought out? Exploration requires you to keep an open mind, but do not believe in something just because you want it to be true.

INQUIRY – Inquiry is the act of asking for information, a probe or query to seek information about a matter of interest. The objective of inquiry is to ask insightful questions. Question everything. Ask why is this so? How can this be better? Where did this information come from? Who is relevant? Why is this information important? Where can I find out more data? What makes this line of inquiry interesting? Questioning is at the heart of investigation.

Voltaire said, "*Judge a man by his questions not by his answers. (Voltaire, 1808)*" Crafting good questions is crucial in all your thinking endeavors. Good questions probe. They launch you on journeys of exploration. Good questions can open new avenues of experimentation. They lead you to a testable hypothesis. Good questions are important in advancing your life objectives, coaxing feedback from others, getting at the heart of a matter, and verifying information.

When you craft questions, determine your objectives. You may be looking for factual answers. You may be seeking an informed opinion. You may need the experience and judgment of an expert. There are probing questions, questions of logic, and questions of exploration. Knowing your purpose for a line of inquiry will help you frame your questions (Fadem, 2008).

In crafting questions ask journalistic questions leading with who, what, when, where, why, how, and to what degree. Questions should elicit thought, and self-examination (Fadem, 2008). Follow-up questions will often be necessary to tease more information from the leading journalistic question. You can employ journalistic questions to dig deeper. Why is that the situation? What makes that so? Why did that happen? When did that occur? Who gave you this information? Follow general questions with specific questions.

Questioning people is an important life skill. Interacting with people requires you to ask questions which engages people. Good questions encourage people to think and engage the person you are having discourse with. Good questions require you to be empathic and to be responsive to others. Listen for information, and probe more. Show empathy to their situation. Be responsive to what the other person is saying and ask relevant follow up questions. Relate questions to a person's frame of reference and their experiences.

In conclusion, the investigation component of Air thinking gets you to delve into your chosen subject with an eye towards creativity. You ask probing questions, to seek out the unknown, and gather ideas. Curiosity will spark your interest to get you to continue searching and thinking. Examination musters your powers of observation on the subject. Experimentation uses tests to examine the validity of a hypothesis, or to determine the efficacy of an idea. Exploration encourages you to seek the unknown. Inquiry helps you formulate good questions.

AIR THINKING – INVESTIGATION		
AIR COMPONENT	PRINCIPLE	DESCRIPTION
INVESTIGATION	Curiosity	Curiosity is the desire to know and learn about something. It is characteristic of inquisitive thinking, exploration, investigation and learning. It represents a thirst for knowledge and mental interest in a subject of inquiry.
	Examination	Examination is a detailed inspection or investigation. The objective is to scrutinize and inspect something. Inspection is the act of carefully examining or scrutinizing something. All your senses and powers of observation are employed.
	Experimentation	Experimentation is the act of conducting a test under controlled conditions to demonstrate a known truth, to examine the validity of a hypothesis, or to determine the efficacy of a process.
	Exploration	Exploration is an analysis of an idea, concept, proposal, subject or theme that is usually unfamiliar to learn more about it.
	Inquiry	Inquiry is the act of asking for information. It is a probe or query to seek information about a matter of

		interest.

Table 15 - Air thinking Investigation component principles

Chapter 11 – Air Thinking and Incubation

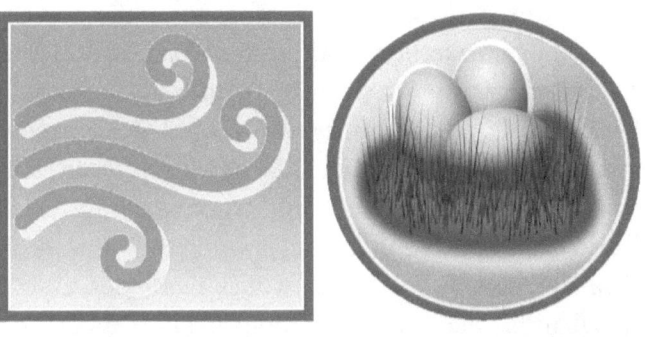

The incubation of an idea is the second component of Air Thinking. The deliberate and passive use of incubation allows your mind to gestate upon a problem. Let this time be a *reculer pour mieux sauter*. This French phrase means "*take a step back to leap forward*". The theorist and psychologist Jay Guilford pointed out that daydreaming, relaxation, meditation, and dream like mental states can stimulate creativity (Guilford, 1967). A period of incubation from mental fatigue can rejuvenate and jump start creativity with a fresh start.

Deliberate incubation starts by deeply studying a problem; then, let the problem rest for a while, and return to it again and with some periodicity. Keep a thinking journal. Whenever something relevant appears for your subject matter, record it. This will eventually stimulate creativity.

Passive incubation allows your mind to contemplate upon a problem without directly working upon it. The mind will continue to work on a problem in the background after you have primed it to think about a problem. Study a problem deeply. Contemplate a solution. Then, take a rest and let your mind wander.

Air swirls around the terrain. Air surrounds us and is ever-present. Similarly, your thinking should encompass a problem. Let your thinking upon a problem swirl about a problem, let it gust and become still. Let your thinking surround an issue, become pervasive and fill your mind. We breathe air and do not think about it. Let your mind approach a problem the same way. Thinking can be in the background, and only when we breathe it in do we become conscious of it.

Graham Wallas noted the importance of incubation during creativity (Wallas, 1926). Many researchers have provided insight into the incubation process. Henri Poincare described the unconscious mechanism whereby the subliminal mind combines mental atoms to form ideas (Poincare, 1929). Woodworth and Schlosberg described the fatigue dissipation mechanism of the incubation process (Woodworth & Schlosberg, 1960). The respite gives the solver time to dispel exhaustion from continuous exertion working on a problem. Herbert Simon noted that in the selective forgetting mechanism, irrelevant material decays in the working memory which allows new, more relevant, more substantial information to accumulate (Simon, 1966). Ilan Yaniv and David Meyer wrote of the external cues mechanism where *"triggers"* stimulate insights necessary for creativity (Yaniv & Meyer, 1987). Karl Duncker noted in the *attention withdrawal* mechanism thinking is diverted, and an impasse is overcome which facilitates a solution (Duncker, 1945). During incubation, the person overcomes false assumptions, restructures problem elements, or represents the problem differently. Pat Langley and Randolph Jones described the prepared mind mechanisms of the incubation creative process (Langley & Jones, 1988). Careful and thorough preparations plant the seeds that allow the mind to ripen a solution. Eliaz Segal wrote of the *returning act* mechanism where the attention of the solver is diverted reducing the effect of false assumptions to unleash creativity (Segal, 2004).

BREAKING CONDITIONING – Conditioning is a kind of learning where a mental association is made between behavior and the consequence of that behavior. Behaviors are reinforced or discouraged through rewards and punishments.

Breaking conditioning is important in incubation because it seeks to break unconscious conditioning. While your mind is working on a problem in the background, conditioning is working to constrict your thinking with preconceived notions. Incubation requires immersion and inquiry into your subject matter. Then, your mind can wade through your topic of interest at its own pace, unconsciously exploring possible solutions.

Breaking condition requires that you take a deep look at your assumptions, your biases and preconceived notions. What assumptions do you hold? What stereotypes do you think you have? Where you disagree with others points to differences in assumptions and background. Areas of contention can reveal hidden conditioning. Culture, media, political opinion, popular culture, and misguided studies can build biases. Political partisanship is a good way to identify some of your prejudices towards a subject. Observe and pay attention to where people have disputes and arguments over something. Very often, each side has some preconceived notions that are influencing their thinking.

CONTEMPLATION – Contemplation is deep reflective thought about a subject. Contemplation is used to incubate ideas through steady reflective thought on a matter. Meditation, reflection, and reverie lie at the heart of creative incubation. The idea of incubation is exposure to a problem or subject of interest and then to allow the mind to explore the subject in the background. Step back and relax.

Meditation is more formal method of calming your mind and body to gain control of turbulence in your thoughts. Meditative techniques will train you to control your breathing, to find a quiet isolated place to practice. Meditation calms the roiling, turbulent ocean of thoughts we all have. Calming the mind will in turn allow your mind to work productively during a creative incubation period.

Reflection is purposeful incubation. You will replay in your mind all the information that you have available. Consider all the available evidence, proposals, and your thoughts on the matter. The idea is to encourage your mind to find new connections and discover new insights on its own.

Reverie is a state of being pleasantly lost in one's thoughts. Daydreaming is one of the common mental states where ideas are incubated. Allowing the mind to wander is a good way to encourage it to find creative solutions. Reverie allows your mind to take your thoughts in random, expansive, or wild directions. Daydreaming is one way to encourage creativity to surface because it is often that carefree dreamy state that allows your creative musings to thrive.

EUREKA EFFECT - In the Greek Language, "*Eureka!*" means, "I have found it!" In 250 BC, a Greek mathematician and physicist named Archimedes coined the term after he discovered a way to measure the volume of King Hieron's crown (Zannos, 2004). As he was lowering himself in a bathtub, he had a sudden flash of inspiration. He realized he could measure the volume of the crown by dunking it in a container full of water. He realized that the amount of water displaced by the crown is equivalent to the amount that overflowed the container. He had a "Eureka!" moment. Archimedes discovered the law of specific gravity and the general science of hydrostatics. This Air technique is a technique focused on stimulating unusual connections and letting the mind stew over a problem. Write down the relevant aspects of your problem and review them regularly. Investigate how other people arrived at solutions to similar problems. Observe how people try to solve the problem. As you regularly review the key aspects of a problem, you are subconsciously directing your brain to mull over the problem in the long-term. You need to gather all the data you can, thereby feeding your subconscious more food for thought. If you germinate your mind with the seeds of the problem, a solution will eventually sprout forth. Your brain will naturally find moments to think about a problem while you are doing other things. It will also chew on the problem as you sleep. You will eventually have a "Eureka!" moment, where a sudden flash of inspiration will tackle you, producing a solution. The Eureka moment occurs when a solution comes knocking unexpectedly. You can incubate ideas by exploring novel approaches, gathering data, giving your mind time to mull over the problem, look for unusual combinations, stimulate your creativity, study proposals, visualize a solution, and use the other Air thinking techniques. As you continue to study, your mind will consider the problem from different angles. You will develop new perspectives that will help you figure out a viable solution. The word *serendipity* is also used to describe a solution that arrives unbidden. You only need to be keen enough to recognize it as a feasible solution.

PROBLEM REFORMULATION – One resourceful way to tackle an issue is to redefine it. Good thinkers value alternate ways to formulate a problem. This results from the fact that our initial perspectives change as we garner more information and become familiar with the situation. We often see what we have been conditioned to see. Develop the habit of expressing problems in as many ways as you can. Redefinition is an important tool in the creativity toolbox. Careful expression of problem or issue will help you break out of familiar patterns, broaden perspectives, defeat limiting habits, conserve flexibility, and open new lines of thought. There are two categories to consider: problems and issues.

A problem is an unacceptable situation, or a situation you want to improve. Problems are best phrased with a "How?" question. How can this problem be addressed? Good thinkers see beyond the initial conception of a problem. The first phrasing of the problem is often unrefined or biased. Creativity looks at the situation in a way that transforms doubt into possibility. Try to express the problem in as many ways as you can think of. Replace vague terms with exact ones. This focuses your problem definition. Look at the situation from different perspectives. Poor thinkers see failure; good thinkers see opportunity. Successful people are committed even in the face of adversity, risks, and unknowns.

The second category for consideration is <u>issues</u>. An issue is a matter that informed people disagree upon. An issue is a question raised for inquiry, and consideration. Resolving an issue requires deciding on which viewpoint is the most reasonable. Issues are best expressed using "*Is*", "*Does*", or "*Should*" as leading words. Phrase issues so that key points are disputed. One technique is to identify the main points of each viewpoint. Then, phrase each main point into a question. Rephrase the issue for clarity. Good thinkers are sensitive to the implications of their assertions. They anticipate, and address arguments that arise.

UNCONVENTIONAL THINKING – Thinking unconventionally incubates ideas because thinking about an issue in a different way than you normally do takes you down avenues that you would not normally explore. This turns out to be a source of innovation.

Unconventional thinking breaks from tradition. Conventional thinking produces the same solutions that everyone else has already come up with. Hence, they are conventional and widely accepted as the proper way to do something. However, innovation requires that you shatter those norms. Be willing to embrace change and break from commonly accepted practices.

Unconventional thinking is good for incubating ideas because it encourages you to break out of thinking ruts. It lets you break from tradition and gets you to be willing to entertain new ideas. Unconventional thinking coaxes you to think outside of the box, and to step outside of your comfort zone. Conventional thinking is safe and comforting. Routine patterns trap your thinking. Innovation and creativity often require you to break from conventional thinking, from protocol.

In conclusion, the incubation component of Air thinking is fostered by breaking conditioning, contemplation, the Eureka effect, problem reformulation, and unconventional thinking. Breaking conditioning requires the self-introspection of questioning your preconceived notions. Contemplation puts your mind into a reflective state of mind which encourages creative thought. The Eureka effect is the sudden flash of insight to spark a creativity. Problem reformulation encourages you to redefine your subject matter, to question why you are studying the matter at hand. Unconventional thinking can play an important role in incubation because it inspires you try new solutions that you would not have otherwise considered with orthodox ordinary solutions.

AIR THINKING – INCUBATION		
AIR COMPONENT	**PRINCIPLE**	**DESCRIPTION**
INCUBATION	Breaking Conditioning	Conditioning is a kind of learning where a mental association is made between behavior and the consequence of that behavior. Behaviors are reinforced or discouraged through rewards and punishments.
	Contemplation	Contemplation is deep reflective thought about a subject. Contemplation is used to incubate ideas through steady reflective thought on a matter.
	Eureka Effect	The Eureka effect is a sudden flash of insight into a problem. This creates a sudden understanding of a previously incomprehensible problem or concept.
	Problem Reformulation	Reformulating the problem statement gets you to question the basis of the analysis. Problem reformulation is the act of redefining the original problem from a different perspective, or approach.
	Unconventional Thinking	Thinking unconventionally incubates ideas because thinking about an issue in a different way that you normally do takes you down avenues that you would not normally explore which can be a source of innovation.

Table 16 - Air thinking Incubation component principles

Chapter 12 – Air Thinking and Insight

Insight is the process of gaining a deeper and greater knowledge into a subject of study. Insight is the third crucial component of creativity. Investigation lays the foundation for understanding and creates the basis from which innovation can sprout. Incubation is the gestation period for new ideas to spring forth after the seeds of creativity have been planted. Insight then is that cultivation that results in a key observation which leads to innovation.

FLEXIBILITY – Mental agility is the ability of your mind to think in new and innovative ways. Flexible thinking is the quality of your mind that lets you think outside the box. It is the creative part of your mind which lets you break a preconceived notion. It is the engine of creativity that produces that flash of insight and the Eureka moment. Mental flexibility is the ability to see the extraordinary in the ordinary and distill the ordinary within the extraordinary.

Insight is the third component of air thinking whereby you are trying to get the insight necessary to produce an innovative and original solution. Gaining the insight necessary to generate an innovative solution requires that your thinking be flexible. You need to have the mental agility to make that leap from the problem formulation to an innovative solution taking into consideration the available evidence.

Can mental agility be honed? Can mental flexibility be practiced? Mental flexibility is developed by keeping an open mind and willingness to entertain new ideas. Practicing brainstorming and the other creative techniques of Air thinking will get you to think unconventionally. If you practice rapid idea generation, you will learn to sharpen your creative thinking skills. Mental flexibility requires that you be familiar with the subject matter to be able to generate new insights that are meaningful. The principles of investigation and incubation also improve your ability to think in innovative ways.

INTUITION – Intuition is the ability to understand something without conscious thought or reasoning. The term is derived from the Latin verb *intuen* which translates to "*look inside*" or "*contemplate*". Intuition is an inspired perception leading to insight. It is one of the qualities of creativity and originality that is characteristic of human intelligence. Intuition provides conclusions and judgments that one would not have otherwise been able to easily arrive at through rational thinking.

Intuition is the subject of psychological study because it is a unique gift of the mind. It is often associated with right brain thinking because of its ties to aesthetics and creativity. It is often attributed to creativity and scientific discovery because of the flash of insight which produces a Eureka solution which would have been otherwise unattainable or difficult to reach through reasoning. Intuition can be a valuable ally on your thinking journey. Learn to pay attention to your intuition.

Intuition may not be easily developed through any methodical technique. However, you can provide the right circumstances for your mind to take that mental leap. Preparation, study, training, investigation, immersion, and the other principles of Air thinking can provide a springboard for your mind to jump to a solution which would have been difficult to arrive at through conventional thinking. One form of intuition is educated guessing. If you sow the seeds of mental success, nourish your mind with preparation, give your mind incubation time for ideas to germinate, your mind will naturally think of solutions to problems. Intuition is nurtured by being in the right place at the right time, circumstances which promote clarity of thought, mental preparation, relevant evidence, and clear-sighted judgment. All the techniques and principles of Air thinking foster creativity and stimulates your intuitive capabilities.

There are those who are physically endowed with great strength, agility, and stamina. There are natural geniuses and those who have great intuitive capabilities. However, within each of us is some capacity for intuitive insight. Intuition is a characteristic shared by all humans. The ability to make a leap of insight to come to a solution without proof is a human endowment. It is a process of the subconscious working behind the scenes to come to a solution through a flash of insight.

Intuition can serve as a beacon, lighting a path for discovery and creativity. Immerse yourself in your chosen subject matter. Identify relevant evidence to your problem through the techniques of Earth thinking. Stimulate your creativity by Air thinking. Intuition will naturally deliver insight with the proper mental cultivation.

Serendipity is also fostered by using intuition. Serendipity is the development of events by chance that yield positive or beneficial results. In this case, happenstance events produce an insightful observation or idea. Luck sometimes plays a role in acts of creativity. Serendipity can inspire ideas.

While you might not be able to develop or train your luck, you can prepare your mind to best capitalize on an unexpected find. In the second century BC, the playwright Terence wrote *"fortis fortuna adiuvat"* which means *"fortune favors the bold"*. In 1854, the chemist and pioneer of the germ theory of disease, Louis Pasteur said *"Dans les champs de l'observation le hasard ne favorise que les esprits prepares"* from French this translates to "in the fields of observation chance favors the prepared mind." This has also been translated more simply to "chance favors the prepared mind." Preparation is the mother of creativity (Pasteur, 1854).

There are three basic pieces of serendipity that come together. The first is that you must be prepared. You need to be well versed in your problem, receptive to new ideas, knowledgeable in the subject matter, and have used the investigation component of Air thinking. The second is that you run across the lucky find. Intuition or a sudden flash of insight might produce this lucky find. Serendipity, by definition, has an element of chance to it. Being in the right place at the right time, talking to knowledgeable people and being prepared increases your chance that serendipity will strike. The last piece is that you need to be able to recognize when an opportunity presents itself. A solution might fall into your lap, but if you do not recognize it as such, it will bypass you.

Serendipity itself is not a technique or a skill which you can hone. Dedicating yourself to be the best at what you do promotes Serendipity. Be knowledgeable, curious, inquisitive, dedicated, and passionate about your subject matter. Let your intuition guide you to solutions that others overlook. You need to explore, experiment and engage the experts. Seek out aficionados. Travel to events for your chosen discipline. "Fortunate" individuals are "lucky" because they are at the right place, at the right time, addressing the right problem, and investigating the right issue. They frequent events where opportunities present themselves.

Suppose Steve is interested in designing a computer application. He has done his homework. He knows how to program a computer. He has a worked towards a degree in computer science. He has always loved to tinker with electronics. He won science fairs as a child. He is well versed in the subject and reads voraciously. He attends conferences and has friends who also enjoy developing applications. He has developed an intuition for solving computer related problems. His skill and experience serve as a fountain of ideas for computer programming. Then, one day he has a conversation with someone who owns a company who offers him a position. Was that a lucky circumstance? Was that serendipity? Of course, it was. However, it was also the pieces of a puzzle falling into place one at a time. The autobiography of Steve Jobs in his book iWoz (Wozniak & Smith, 2007) is a good example of intuition and serendipity leading to insights.

MENTAL FLUENCY – Mental Fluency is ease of cognition. It is a measure of how easily experiences, information, and decisions can be processed.
Mental fluency is developed by experience, mental acuity, technique, and knowledge. Someone who is very experienced in a subject, activity, or discipline will process new information more effectively or efficiently than a rookie.

Mental acuity and sheer mental aptitude can allow someone to process new information from foreign situations quickly. Mental agility grants someone the ability to think faster and make quicker decisions. Mental facility is a natural aptitude to learn something well and easily. Most people have their strengths and weaknesses. You should discover your gifts and aptitudes and build upon them.

Mental fluency can be promoted through technique. Many of the components of air thinking and the practice of air thinking are aimed at improving your mental fluency. Continual practice with the elements of thinking will enhance your ability to process experiences and information related to your subject of interest. The evidence component of Earth thinking, and investigation component of Air thinking will improve your familiarity of a subject and build a knowledge base. Fire thinking techniques are aimed at improving your ability to make efficient decisions. Water thinking techniques will improve your ability to process information and experiences.

Knowledge is another factor that can improve mental fluency. The more information you have about a subject, the better the chance that you will run across something that is familiar. You will be able to place new information better in an existing framework of understanding. Understanding the big picture allows you to see where a new piece of the puzzle fits. A deep knowledge of a subject of interest will allow you to incorporate new information with greater efficiency because it is less likely that you will run across information that is completely unfamiliar to you.

When information is unfamiliar it requires conscious thought, analysis, and logical reasoning to process. There is nothing wrong with using your mental faculties, but the processing does take time.

COMPARISON (SIMILARITY & DIFFERENCES) – Looking for elements of commonality or areas of differences can germinate an idea. They can serve as starting points for thinking journeys and new paths to explore.
Finding patterns, similarities and differences is one of the primary functions of Water thinking. Identifying commonalities between things or spotting differences can often be the crucial catalyst for a key insight.

Finding commonalities can produce insights because you may see how two disparate things can be related to one another. Predictive characteristics may prove useful if you have identified a new piece of information as belonging to a specific class or category of things. Object oriented software programming was developed to identify commonalities between things and classify them into objects to be modeled by software. Aside from predictions and modeling, finding commonalities may also give you a way to determine how effective or efficient a solution might be.

As an example of seeing how similarities can be used to produce insights, consider some of the strangest mammals that have ever been discovered. These mammals include the star-nose mole, pangolin, tree sloth, duck billed platypus, Indus river dolphin, naked mole rat, wrinkle-faced bat, narwhal, marsupial mole, pink fair armadillo, and the slow Loris. None of these animals appear to be mammals. The researchers who have studied these animals have identified characteristics which have classified them as mammals. Mammals are warm blooded, have vertebrae, typically have hair or fur, secrete milk by mothers nursing young, and typically give live birth. Having this framework in mind has allowed researchers to see insights about how these animals behave and live because they share traits in common to all mammals.

In conclusion, flexibility, intuition, mental fluency, and similarity are important principles of the insight component of Air thinking. These principles help generate creative insight because they stimulate your ability to find a creative solution. Mental flexibility allows you to think in new and novel ways. It is your capacity to think unconventionally. Intuition is the ability to understand something without conscious reasoning. Mental fluency is a measure of how efficiently and quickly you can process new experiences, information, and decisions. Similarities and differences generate insight by giving you predictive qualities, common characteristics, and new mental models to work with.

AIR THINKING – INSIGHT		
AIR COMPONENT	**PRINCIPLE**	**DESCRIPTION**
INSIGHT	Flexibility	Mental agility is the ability of your mind to think in new and innovative ways.
	Intuition	Intuition is the ability to understand something without conscious thought or reasoning. Intuition can produce an insightful observation or an innovative idea. Intuition helps you take advantage of serendipity.
	Mental Fluency	Mental Fluency is the ease of cognition. It is a measure of how easily experiences, information, and decisions can be processed.
	Comparison (Similarity & Difference)	Looking for elements of commonality or areas of differences can germinate an idea. They can serve as starting points for thinking journeys and new paths to explore. Similarities and differences generate insight by giving you predictive qualities, common characteristics, and new mental models to work with.

Table 17 - Air thinking Insight component principles

Chapter 13 – Air Thinking and Innovation

The Air element of thinking innovation component chapter is laid out differently than the other Air thinking component chapters. This component of Air thinking does not use a step-by-step methodical method. Instead, the innovation component of Air thinking has a tool chest of techniques to stimulate innovation and creativity. If one technique doesn't work, you can pull out another to get your ideas flowing. Use one technique and if that is not fruitful, use another one. The more ideas you produce, the better the chances of having good ones. The important thing is to generate as many ideas as you can. The golden rule to creative thinking is not to evaluate ideas during the idea generation stage.

BRAINSTORMING - In 1939, a team led by advertising executive Alex Osborn coined the term *brainstorm*. The method uses the brain to storm a problem in a commando-like fashion, with each participant attacking the same objective. Later, he wrote the book called Applied Imagination (Osborn, 1953). Osborn claimed that people can double their idea production with brainstorming (Osborn, 1953). The basic ground rules for brainstorming are:

A. **QUANTITY** – The emphasis during idea generation should be on quantity of ideas created not quality of ideas. Participants should try to generate as many ideas as possible during a brainstorming session by noting any idea that comes to their mind no matter how silly it seems. Timed sessions can be setup where participants focus on rapid idea generation to stimulate creativity.

B. **ORIGINALITY** – Brainstorming participants should be encouraged to come up with unusual ideas. Zany, unorthodox, and outlandish ideas are welcome during a brainstorming session. The generation of an unusual idea may help you create more ideas. Unusual ideas spur on creativity. It helps to stimulate sparks of insight those uniquely human leaps of insight that give birth to great ideas.

Originality is the ability to think uniquely. It is characterized by novel and innovative ideas. It has a unique style and substance. Originality is associated with the creativity of artists, writers, painters, inventors, musicians, and thinkers.

C. **COLLABORATION** - Participants should combine and improve their ideas. Let ideas flow, merge, and build from one another. Participants should be encouraged to use the idea of one person as a springboard for more ideas. If a suggestion opens a new avenue of thought, people should explore it.

D. **SUSPEND JUDGMENT** - Criticism and judgment should be ruled out during the idea generation process. The evaluation of ideas should be deferred to a later stage of the problem-solving process. Offner, Kramer, and Winter (Offner, Kramer, & Winter, 1996) suggested that using trained facilitators who are familiar with the rules of brainstorming increase creative productivity.

COLLABORATIVE CREATIVITY - There are many times where you will need to work with other people to deliberately generate ideas to solve a problem. When you collaborate with other people you can share ideas and build upon the ingenuity of others. The most famous mechanism for collaborative creativity is brainstorming. Other techniques include brain-writing, brain-sketching, object-based brain storming, analogical reasoning, nominal group technique, the Delphi technique, and playgrounds.

A. **BRAIN-WRITING** - In Brain-writing, people write down their ideas on written notes. They then share them in a round-robin fashion. People can then add or create new ideas as the notes are passed around. The same rules for brainstorming can be applied to brain-writing: quantity of ideas, originality, collaboration, and suspending judgment. Paulus and Yang found productivity gains with this mechanism because it overcomes the problem of production blocking (Paulus & Yang, 2000). Production Blocking occurs because people must take turns talking during a verbal brainstorming session which disrupts individual thinking (Nijstad & Stroebe, 2006). If using computers for Brain-writing, participants would pass digital notes. Brain-writing facilitates the suspension of judgment while still maximizing creative collaboration. Thus, this is a good technique if the people you are working with have a hard time suspending judgment and are quick to criticize new ideas.

B. **BRAIN-SKETCHING** – Brain-sketching was created by Van Gundy (Van Gundy, 1988). In this technique, the participants use drawing, and sketches to generate ideas. Brainstorming is a sentential, or verbal activity. Brain-writing uses written language. Brain-sketching employs the visual skills of the participants and develops ideas using sketches. The basic brain-storming process of generating ideas, collaboration, focus on originality, quantity of ideas, and suspension of judgment still applies. Brain-sketching is a technique that engages the spatial and creative aspect of your brain. Do not worry if your drawings are crude. Use a minimal amount of words and lettering, use words only to highlight abstract ideas or to enhance your drawings. Pass around the pictures with your collaborators to allow others to build upon your pictures. Draw quickly and crudely to generate a quantity of ideas, let your drawings build upon themselves.

C. **OBJECT BASED BRAIN-STORMING** - Object-based brainstorming was proposed by Vidal, Mulet, and Gomez-Senent (Vidal, Mulet, & Gomez-Senent, 2004). This technique uses the four basic guidelines of a brain-storming session. The primary difference is that physical objects are used during the session. Vidal et al. suggested using MECCANO components and pieces. Building blocks, clay, toys, or other props could serve as your creative aides (Vidal, Mulet, & Gomez-Senent, 2004). Their investigation shows that design problems of a functional kind are effectively explored using object-based brainstorming. Objects can absorb, bounce, connect, float, fly, hit, melt, merge, move, roll, spin, split, and twist. Using physical objects is valuable in the creative process because it encourages you to think spatially in four dimensions. Each of the brainstorming techniques appeals to different mental skills. Brainstorming capitalizes on verbal language skills. Brain-writing employs written skills. Brain-sketching uses visualization; and object-based brainstorming uses kinesthetic perception.

D. **ANALOGICAL REASONING** – The power of analogy during problem solving should not be underestimated. Using the solution from one problem and putting the basic concepts to use in another field is an effective means to stimulate creativity. Thompson, Lowenstein, and Gentner defined *analogical reasoning* as the process of taking a concept from one domain and applying it to another domain (Thompson, Loewenstein, & Gentner, Avoiding Missed Opportunities in

Managerial Life: Analogical Training More Powerful than Individual Case Training, 2000). A deep understanding of the structural similarities is required to transfer ideas from one field to another specialty. Thus, analogical reasoning can also be a rich source of ideas. The difficulty of applying previously learned knowledge to new situations is called the *inert knowledge problem*. To use analogical reasoning look for problems that are similar to the one you are considering. Then study how other people developed a solution. If you have the opportunity, discuss directly with those original thinkers to learn more.

E. **NOMINAL GROUP TECHNIQUE & THE DELPHI TECHNIQUE** – The nominal group technique was proposed by Van de Ven, and Delbecq (Van de Ven & Delbecq, 1974). The *Nominal group* technique begins with a brain-storming session. The ideas are subsequently shared by the group in a round-robin fashion. The ideas are collected, gathered, and summarized. The group discusses the ideas to gain clarity and understanding. Then each person rank-orders and evaluates the resultant ideas. The *Delphi* Technique is a variation of the Nominal group technique where the participants do not interact face-to-face. A facilitator distributes the topic to each member and asks for responses. The facilitator then collects the responses and solicits feedback. The process is repeated until a solution is produced. This method is conducive to geographically dispersed members.

F. **PLAYGROUND** – Thompson suggested that work playgrounds can instill motivation and stimulate creativity (Thompson, Improving the Creativity of Organizational Work Groups, 2003). The idea is to set aside physical space where people can play and innovate. Innovation spaces are where people can play, experiment, and test ideas. Guided by functionality, the playground should have objects which encourage thinking. You can set aside a space in your home to use as an Exploratorium. This would be a space that encourages and fosters creativity by engaging you to play and explore.

GEDANKEN – A *Gedanken experiment* is a thought exercise. It is a test of a concept or idea carried out mentally. Gendanken experiment is a mental exercise which can be used in lieu of a physical experiment. They can be used for a variety of purposes. In ancient Greek philosophy, the *deiknymi*, or though experiment, was used as a method for mathematical proof. In 1812, Hans Christian Orsted coined the term Gedanken experiment to define an exercise where the mind is used to imagine the result of physical experiment. As with many experiments, Gedanken exercises are often aimed at challenging a conventional theory, confirming a prevailing theory, establishing a new theory, or replacing an existing theory with a new one.

There are seven types of Gedanken experiments: pre-factual, counter-factual, semi-factual, prediction, hind-casting, retro-diction, and back-casting (Yeates, 2004). *Pre-factual* thought experiments speculate on a possible future outcome given the occurrence of a specific event. *Counter-factual* gedanken experiments theorize on the possible outcomes of a different past. *Semi-factual* thought experiments consider the likelihood of a present state given a different past. *Predictive* experiments anticipate a future outcome from a set of circumstances and actions. *Hind-casting* tests the validity of a model simulation after an event has already occurred. *Retro-diction* tries to establish the cause of a specific event by moving backwards in time. Reverse engineering and forensics in science are examples of retro-diction. *Back-casting* takes an imaginary future outcome and moves backwards in time step-by-step until the present is reached. The purpose of back-casting is to determine the mechanisms by which the future could be attained from the present.

INNOVATION FACTORS – In this technique, you are deliberately trying to generate new ideas. The following are 32 innovation factors to help you think outside the box. These are 32 fundamental idea seeds get you to think about your problem in a new light. They are adapted from my first book "*32 Innovation Factors*" (Cheung, 32 Innovation Factors, 2003). A condensed description of the factors is given here. A full account is given in the four elements of thinking full edition. An entire book devoted to them in my "*32 Innovation Factors*".

A. **ADAPTIVE** – The adaptive factor deals with the ability to change to new circumstances, or to change to a different purpose or function.
B. **APERTURE** – An aperture is a portal. It serves as the gateway into a system. Try changing the input. Vary the arrival, cost, quantity, quality, shape, size, or type of things that are used as part of your solution.
C. **BOUNDARY** – Think about the boundaries of your problem. What are the limits of your problem? Why are they limits? What containers can you use? What form, or shape best suits your problem?
D. **BUFFER** – A buffer is something that is used between the system and the external environment. Is it possible to put something between the system and the external environment that can be used?

E. **CELLULAR** – The cellular factor employs individual units as part of a larger system. Can a system be broken down into components? What parts can form into wholes? Think about your problem in piecemeal.

F. **CHANNEL** –How can sharing be used in the solution? How can you incorporate the concept of sharing into your solution? How can you break down your problem such that multiple people can partake?

G. **COMPOSITE** –This factor merges two or more things together into a new, emergent thing. Can two things be merged together in your problem? Can some aspects, characteristics, or parts of two things be blended together?

H. **CYCLES** – Cycles are anything that repeats in time. Cycles have been used to clock, monitor, poll, select, switch, synchronize, time, transform, and trigger things. See if there are patterns that repeat in your problem.

I. **EPICENTER** – The epicenter factor is defined as the central focus of a system, the point of control or the focus of a process. Identify the core ideas of the system from which other things radiate outward from.

J. **FEEDBACK** – Feedback uses a result or output as an input. Feedback is one of the most useful concepts in nature and engineering. Most systems that balance equilibriums utilize feedback.

K. **FILTERING** – Filtering selectively passes some elements while blocking other things. Filters are used to compartmentalize, correlate, eliminate disturbances, find patterns, group, isolate, polarize, refine inputs, and separate flows.

L. **FUZZY** – The fuzzy factor is about shades of grey. Can you find a middle ground that will work? Can a compromise be reached between two opposite parts of your problem? Is there a midpoint between two extremes in your problem? I

M. **INTEGRATED** – Integrating two or more things together relates them. This factor brings pieces of a puzzle together to form a big picture. Integrated concepts, systems, or components come together to make a working whole.

N. **INTERCHANGEABLE** – This factor relates to elements in a system which can be exchanged for another. What things can you swap out? What parts of your problem can be exchanged for something else?

O. **LAYERED** – The layer factor is a band or coating. Layers are prevalent in nature. It may be useful to introduce or to remove a layer. A layer can take many forms (both physical and conceptual).

P. **MATCHING** – This factor identifies complementary opposites. Are there some complementary opposites in your problem? Is there a matching part that would be useful to use? Look for dynamic interactions in your solution.

Q. **MODULARITY** – A module can be something which has a well-defined interface and is well delineated (or encapsulated). Look for a way to isolate a part of your problem. Perhaps that part can be subcontracted or outsourced.

R. **MODULATED** – The Modulated innovation factor regulates, adjusts, and adapts things. Ask yourself, where are the bottlenecks in the problem? Why do the bottlenecks exist? What constraints are there in your system?

S. **MULTIPLEXED** – This factor involves interweaving things together. Often, a solution can interweave elements together. Can you make things take turns to share a resource? What is the most efficient way to intermingle elements together?

T. **NETWORKED** – The Network factor deals with connectivity. Consider how networking can be used to generate ideas for your problem. How can I use my connections to help me solve my problem?

U. **QUANTIZED** – The quantized factor relates to the discrete magnitude values used to describe a quantity. Precise measurements facilitate description, exactness, interchangeability, manufacturability, repeatability, and reproducible consistency.

V. **REPRESENTATION** – The representation factor deals with a logical, virtual, or proxy representation of something. What represents my problem the best? Can you use a substitute? Will a proxy serve instead of the actual thing?

W. **RESONANCE** – Resonance refers to phenomena where waves reinforce each other. Resonance is created in many ways: by splashing, compressing, blowing, funneling, focusing, squeezing, and pulsing something. What things amplify each another? What components of your problem resonate together?

X. **SCALING** – Scaling allows something to grow or shrink without changing its true nature. The basic idea of the scaling factor is to amplify, magnify, attenuate, or boost. What things need to be amplified, magnified or boosted? Some scalable things: dimension, energy, ideas, images, money, proportion, sound, and time.

Y. **SIGNATURE** – The signature factor represents security measures in your solution. Is security important to your problem? What parts of the problem need to use identification? Do parts of your system that need security?

Z. **SWARM** – This factor deals with a quantity of specialists over the quality of generalists. Generalists are few, costly, indispensable, high performance units. Specialists are numerous, efficient, inexpensive, disposable, special purpose units.

AA. **SWITCHING** – This factor deals with switching between alternatives. The idea of switching includes alternating functions, changing roles, selecting amongst choices, swapping things, transmuting something, and turning on or off.

BB. **SYMBIOSIS** – The symbiosis factor deals with a mutually beneficial relationship between two things. There are four basic types of symbiosis: commensalism, parasitism, mutualism, and endosymbiosis/ecto-symbiosis.

CC. **SYMMETRY** – Two things have symmetry if they form a complementary mirror image of each other. You can use symmetry in your problem by using a counterpart. Is there a matching pattern? Interlocking gears have symmetry.

DD. **TRANSIENT** – A transient is a short-lived phenomenon. What things are not permanent? What things are transitory? What could appear and disappear without notice? What events come and go in your problem?

EE. **TRIGGERING** – A trigger causes another event to occur. Cause and effects (causal chains) are triggers. A means to an end creates sequences of cause and effects. Consider what causes could induce some events to happen?

FF. **WAVES** – Waves are a cascade of things that permeate the environment. Learn how to identify, manipulate, and isolate waves. Biorhythms, daily cycles, flows and ebbs, Tidal forces, waxing and waning, can be used to your advantage.

VISUALIZATION - Visualization uses your mind's eye to picture images relevant to your problem. Action is always preceded by thought. An architect has a concept of a design in his mind and before he drafts a blueprint for the home. The idea is like a blueprint, it creates an image of the form, which can then manifest itself into a physical form. With visualization, we can stimulate creativity, and picture solutions. Visualization applies to a process where you use your imagination to give mental form to a concept.

There are six basic steps for effective visualization:

A. **SET A GOAL** – First, you will focus on a goal to think about. The goal could be a problem, something you want to create, or a personal goal. It can be any topic, concept, thing or idea.

B. **DETAILS** – Next, make a mental picture of the object or situation that you chose as your goal. Then, close your eyes for a few minutes and relax. Expand on the initial thought and include as many details as you can. Consider the qualities of the subject. Some qualities to consider are color, condition, features, form, function, history, labels, make, manufacturer, model, name, owner, relationships, size, title, value and volume. Then, draw a physical picture of the subject. Even if you are not a very good artist, just try it. Get your thoughts down in writing.

C. **FOCUS** – Focus on the chosen subject through study, practice, and concentration. Once you have a goal and a picture of it, you can review it regularly.

This will reinforce your visualization of the problem. It will become more of a reality for you. It will take mental form. Have the concept in focus to allow you to refine it further and reinforce the idea.

D. **INTEGRATE** – You can use the other Air thinking techniques with visualization to help energize your creativity. Then integrate in the other elements of thinking, this will help you refine your idea further. Integrate your ideas, maps, pictures, visualizations, concepts, doodles and images into your proposed solutions. Visualization will help you generate ideas and solutions because it can bring a tangible quality to a concept. It should be used in conjunction with other methods to stimulate your creativity.

E. **DRAW** – Take a few moments and capture your visualization on paper or in a computer. It doesn't matter if you are not a good artist. The picture is meant only as a mental trigger for you. The vital thing is that you have depicted the subject that you have been focusing on. Now, doodle, explore and diagram freely. Explore variations and refinements to your ideas. Feel free to draw flowcharts, cartoons, storyboards, scribbles, panoramic vistas, or anything that is appropriate to your problem. Let your drawings stimulate your creativity.

F. **REVIEW** – Remember to come back to your visualizations and objectives. Goals often change before they are developed into a physical reality. That is a natural part of the thinking process. This is how we change, learn and grow. Acknowledge that the visualization you created will change. Allow it to adapt so that it can fit into the big picture of your life. Over time, your original visualization changes its relationship to your current problems. As old problems get solved, they open visualizations for new beginnings. After you successfully use visualization, acknowledge this accomplishment. After you have reviewed your visualizations, return to the first step and begin to explore anew. Visualization uses active contemplation through images to generate creative solutions.

In conclusion, the objective of the innovation component of Air thinking draws upon a variety of techniques to develop ideas. The investigation, incubation, and insight components have set the stage for the creative process to flourish. Brainstorming and collaborative creativity are used to stimulate ideas by working in a team or with a partner. A *gedanken* is a thought exercise which can be carried out in lieu or in preparation for an actual experiment. The innovation factors spur on creativity. Visualization employs mental imagery to assist in the creative process. These principles are tools in your creative toolbox to inspire and coax original thinking. Their frequent use will develop your creative abilities.

AIR THINKING – INNOVATION		
AIR COMPONENT	**PRINCIPLE**	**DESCRIPTION**
INNOVATION	Brainstorm	Brainstorming is a specific technique for idea generation.
	Collaborative Creativity	Collaborative creativity is the act of working together with another person or with a group to stimulate innovation, imagination, and inventiveness.
	Gedanken	A Gedanken experiment is a thought exercise. It is a test of a concept or idea carried out mentally which can produce insights and new avenues of exploration.
	Innovation factors	Methodical and deliberate idea generation can produce innovation. This is the intentional and conscious practice of generating ideas.
	Visualization	Visualization is mental imagery that is a representation of the physical world. Memory models play a vital role in memory and thinking. Visualization can be used to affect your thoughts, abilities, and expectations.

Table 18 - Air thinking Innovation component principles

Chapter 14 – Water Thinking and Linking

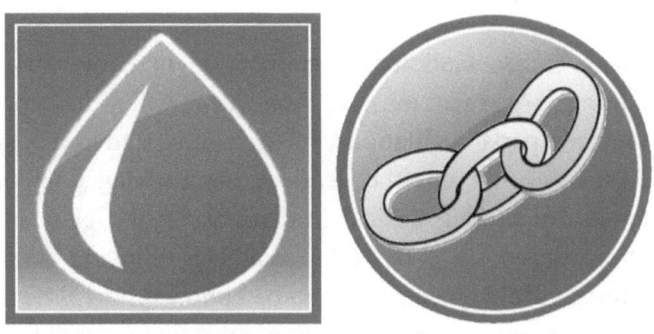

The aspect of thinking represented by the Water Symbol is synthesis thinking. Water thinking is used to find important associations, interactions and patterns. One of the objectives of synthesis thinking is to see how ideas can combine. The use of synthesis thinking produces recognition of the big picture and an understanding of the broader context of a subject matter. Water thinking allows you to understand the ecosystem in which concepts thrive and how the individual ideas fit into their environment. The ability to relate two concepts and organize them into new patterns or fit them into a mental architecture only comes with a deep insight into a field of study.

Using synthesis thinking will identify interactions between parts of a system and highlight how they integrate. By opening your mind to new possibilities, you will see many uses for synthesis thinking. Finding these critical interactions will allow you to methodically consider a system or problem. Synthesis thinking connects ideas together. It is used to see the big picture, to understand the context and environment better. This is accomplished through methodical examination of your subject matter and deliberately looking for meaningful associations. When you find associations between ideas, you will more easily see the big picture, which can facilitate the creation of plans and strategies.

Water thinking can be used in problem solving. The goal of Water thinking during problem solving is to uncover links between parts of your problem that you might not have considered when you first formulated your problem. It can be used to compartmentalize or modularize your solution. Identifying linkages helps problem solving. They provide new alternatives and insights that were not obvious but are important. Networking ideas will give you new perspectives.

Association, Cross-fertilization, decomposition, organization, and patterns are the basis for linking component of water thinking. You will find these principles to be invaluable mental tools.

ASSOCIATION – An association is a connection or cooperative link between people, places, things, organizations, or concepts. Alliances, coalitions, puzzle pieces, interchangeable parts, affiliations, relationships, and bonds are examples of associations. Associating ideas is the heart of the Linking component. You can identify associations by finding critical links between the elements of a system. Finding associations serves as a basis for synthesis thinking because when you understand how things are connected, a web of knowledge will develop (Barabasi, 2014). That web is the key to forming a big picture understanding of your subject which facilitates understanding of how ideas combine.

There are many ways that you can find associations between ideas. Associations can be based on: action, behavior, causality, common knowledge, concept, chronological relationships, family relationships, function (dynamic attributes), geographical location, relationship by issues, personal motivations, physical properties (static attributes), policy, practice, price, procedure, quality, strategy and value. These are only a few of the possible associations between concepts and ideas. Many more association types are conceivable that can be tailored to the study of your subject. Additionally, Wells identified several ways that concepts might be associated (Wells, 1911). These ways include egocentric, egocentric predicate (example lonesome - stranded), evaluation (rose - beautiful), matter of fact predicate (spinach - green), judgment of quality, simple predicate, subject relation (dog - bite), object relation (dog – bone), causality, coordination, subordination, supra-ordination, contrast, coexistence, identity, and assonance.

One of the possible associations is based in temporal relationships. In the case of a chronological organization, ideas and events usually have a causal relationship. Causal relationships organize information, which improves your understanding of a subject. Causal relationships help you think about a subject and are a way to associate concepts.

Some linkages will be obvious, while others will be subtle. It will be helpful to identify the obvious associations first, and then identify the subtle ones. Keep in mind, that you can probably force an artificial association between any two ideas or concepts. Air thinking encourages finding outlandish associations to stimulate creativity. However, Water thinking strives to find relevant and meaningful connections.

CROSS-FERTILIZATION – This principle is used in the sense of cross-fertilization of ideas. Taking concepts from one field or discipline and applying them to a different one. The cross-fertilization creates a link between two fields of study. Inter-disciplinary studies such as biomedical engineering, which crosses the biomedical field with engineering, are an example of cross-fertilization of ideas.

Analogy is a verbal (writing) example of cross-fertilization. Analogy takes one concept in one field and applies it to another via verbal expression to help understand a concept. Cross-fertilization provides a way to synthesize ideas, merges fields of study, and blends concepts. Drawing an analogy lets the mind quickly see how an idea used in one area can be shifted for use into another. An analogy to help understand analogies is like a cooking tool such as a butter knife used for gardening. The analogy is like a tool such as a butter knife, originally used to spread butter or jam, cross-fertilized into a different purpose such as digging up soil.

The experience, teachings, principles and tools from one discipline of study can be cross fertilized with another. Academic disciplines include algebra, anthropology, archaeology, architecture, astronomy, biology, botany, business administration, chemistry, communication, computer sciences, criminology, earth sciences, economics, education, engineering, geology, history, law, linguistics, literature, mathematics, medicine, philosophy, physics, political science, psychology, sociology, statistics, and zoology. Many cross-fertilization fields have resulted from a merger of two disciplines. Some of these fields of study include biophysics (biology & physics), quantum chemistry (physics & chemistry), bioinformatics (biology & computer sciences), quantum information processing (physics & computer sciences), and biomedical engineering (medical sciences & engineering).

DECOMPOSITION – Decomposition breaks down a complex subject or concept into component elements or simpler constituents. Decomposition assists in comprehension of the interrelationship between elements in a system. The act of trying to decompose, compartmentalize, and stratify a system requires increasing levels of understanding of that system. It also creates conceptual links between the constituent elements.

The principle of decomposition is applied by breaking down a problem into manageable components. If you are examining a system, find logical groupings that work together. Decomposition is used to delimit the essential components of a system. If you are analyzing a conceptual subject, break down the concept into elemental ideas. Identifying the main ideas, and main subsystems allows you to understand how the components interact which is a prelude to synthesis.

Once you have identified the major ideas, subsystems, or components you can analyze the functional aspects. You can decompose a system functionally by grouping subsystems by similar function. Components of a system might be able to be grouped by function. Breaking down a complex problem into manageable, cohesive units will allow you to tackle the problem in pieces. You can break down the problem based on any combination of: concepts, deliverables, finance, form, function, issue, resources, space, or time. Break down a task into steps in a process. Break down a system by functional units. Break down a concept by logical groupings. If you break down a problem into its essential components the problem becomes manageable. An additional benefit is that by decomposing a system you can isolate and analyze one factor at a time. When you break down a boulder, you can move it one rock at a time.

ORGANIZATION – Organization implies a grouping or ordering of concepts, people, or things. Organization of elements, in this case, is employed with the purpose of identifying links between them. In first stages of problem solving, you gathered, organized, and evaluated your data. Organization can reveal the association and links between elements in a problem.

As you proceed with Water thinking, you will want to examine the organization of your data. The reason for this is that your perspective on the problem will change as you apply the elements of thinking. New associations and insights will evolve your perspective about the problem. Organization of information requires logical choices, selection of organization category, associations between groups of information, and an information scaffold. There are usually different ways to organize data based on these choices that you make. Different associations and links will be important based on the kind of organization you make. Organizing information associates the principle ideas in your subject of interest.

There are many ways to organize your information. The ways you can organize information include: action, behavior, conceptual, chronological, function (dynamic attributes), issue, location, physical properties (static attributes), policy, price, strategy, and topic.

Summarizing may also assist in organizing information. When you study a subject, take some time to reflect and summarize what you have learned. Identify the key concepts, and structure of information that was presented. For Water thinking, organizing information is used to help synthesize ideas and information. You are looking for links and associations to find new applications, new insights, and new ideas. If you have a complex problem with a lot of data, summarize each main concept by using keywords. This will help you see the big picture, allowing you to associate ideas. It may be helpful to tag information to represent your key concepts, particularly if you have a lot of data. Summarize each point on a separate card. Many software programs exist that allow you to summarize your thoughts on individual electronic cards. By summarizing, using key-words, and concept cards, you will be able to lay out the entire problem in front of you. This will facilitate finding meaningful associations.

PATTERNS – A pattern is a recurrent design, or intelligible form of something. A model or design used as a template for other works. Patterns can be a catalyst to synthesis thinking because you can see the big picture and how ideas might combine. Patterns can provide a template or mental scaffolding upon which ideas are nestled. Patterns can be identified by a conscious effort to find meaningful structures within information.

Patterns can be the key to understanding concepts, and the important insight necessary when seeking a solution to a problem. Many kinds of patterns can be used when studying a subject or problem. Patterns can be used for diagrams, designs, art, and décor. Patterns can be mathematical in nature. They are used in art, biology, engineering, history, language, mathematics, and science. Patterns can be conceptual, visual, spatial, or temporal.

Linking ideas together is the bread and butter of Water thinking. It will help you see the big picture and identify important patterns in your chosen subject matter. This, in turn, will help you generate solutions during problem solving. As you apply this skill, you will become better at finding meaningful associations between concepts. You will be able to adapt to changing situations as your mind becomes more adept at Water thinking.

WATER THINKING – LINKING		
WATER COMPONENT	**PRINCIPLE**	**DESCRIPTION**
LINKING	Association	An association is a connection or cooperative link between people, places, things, organizations, or concepts. Alliances, coalitions, puzzle pieces, interchangeable parts, affiliations, relationships, and bonds are examples of associations.
	Cross-Fertilization	Used in the sense of cross-fertilization of ideas. Taking concepts from one field or discipline and applying them to a different one. The cross-fertilization creates a link between two fields of study. Inter-disciplinary studies, such as biomedical engineering, are an example of cross-fertilization of ideas.
	Decomposition	Breaking down a complex subject or concept into component elements or simpler constituents. Decomposition assists in comprehension of the interrelationship between elements in a system. It also creates conceptual links between the constituent elements. As an example, the human body is composed of bone, flesh, skin, blood, organs, and muscle as some of the constituent elements.
	Organization	A grouping, positioning, alignment or ordering of objects, concepts, people, or things with the purpose of identifying links between them.
	Patterns	A pattern is a recurrent design, or intelligible form of something. A model or design used as a template for other works. The blueprint for a home or a technical schematic for a manufactured component are examples of patterns.

Table 19 - Water thinking Linking component principles

Chapter 15 – Water Thinking and Perspective

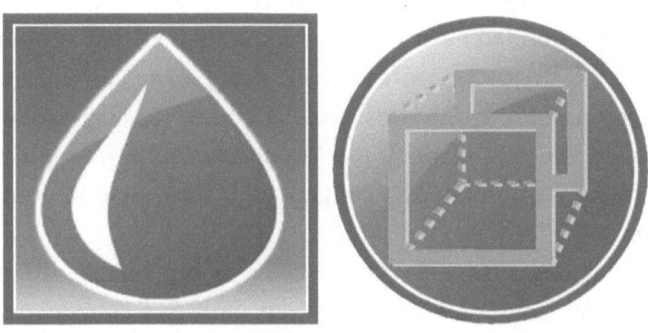

Perspective is the consideration for different points of view. It is a different way of regarding a concept or problem. Perspective is one of the four Water thinking components because the ability to see from different points of view fosters comprehension. Seeing the landscape, big picture, broader context, and environment will often assist in mastery of your problem or chosen subject matter.

The key principles of the perspective component are big picture & maps, ecology & systems, framework, planning, and viewpoints. These principles can be practiced, improving your abilities to see problems from different perspectives. They will be vital in your thinking journeys and a handy ally when trying to use synthesis thinking.

BIG PICTURE & MAPS – The big picture is a diagrammatic representation of a concept showing relevant major features. The perspective component principle of the *big picture* involves understanding the greater context of a problem or subject. The objective is to understand the greater environment upon which elements of your problem are nestled within.

Perhaps one of the simplest yet most effective analogies to using a big picture is the assembly of a jig-saw puzzle. The pieces of the puzzle are joined together to form a big picture. Each piece of the puzzle carries some information of the greater whole. When it is assembled with other pieces it forms a greater whole. Piecing together information to form a big picture can develop a greater perspective.

A map is another way to think about forming a big picture. A map is a diagrammatic representation of a geographical area or a conceptual system. A map is an overview of a geographical area. The purpose of a map is for people to be able to see major and significant features of the landscape. Some features are so large that it can only be observed from the air or space.

The big picture is defined as any over-arching themes that simultaneously apply to all or most of the main concepts in your problem or chosen subject. You are seeking to develop a confederation of ideas. You are looking to identify the forest among the trees. If you can identify the key ideas within your subject of interest, they can serve as the framework, the conceptual pillars, that all your other data can be placed within.

A meta-concept may also help you identify a big picture. Meta-concepts are ideas about the ideas. The meta-concept is an umbrella concept that ties together numerous groupings of ideas. A meta-concept pertains to the concepts about the concepts. A dictionary is an example of a meta-concept because it is a set of words about words. Another example would be an encyclopedia which is a set of concepts about concepts. An overview, summary, glossary, index, table of contents are all meta-concepts aimed as delineating a big picture view of a subject.

The organization of data helps you see the big picture (Gharajedgaghi, 2005). Organization was described as one of the principles of the linking component of Water thinking. If you analyze how and why you choose to organize information, you will see patterns and structures. Consider the choices you made in organizing your information. You should look for meaningful superstructures to the organization of data.

Give yourself time to contemplate the big picture. Do not expect that the big picture will immediately leap out at you. Give your mind time to mull over your subject. In time, you will most likely identify a grand idea that can unify all the pieces of your puzzle into a big picture. Finding a coherent and meaningful big picture will take perseverance and contemplation. Once identified, grand principles can help you refine your understanding.

ECOLOGY & SYSTEMS – The ecology is the relationship of things and their environment. The mental ecology is a system of concepts and their associated context. A system is a set of interdependent connected components forming an integrated complex whole.

In nature, the ecology is the relationship between animals and plants to their surrounding environment. Scientists study the diversity of creatures within an ecosystem, the mass (biomass) and quantity of creatures (population), competition among creatures. Scientists identify ecosystem processes such as production (synthesis of organic compounds), pedogenesis (soil formation), nutrient cycling (the food web), and niche construction (altering the environment) (Molles, 2012).

The identification of an ecology as a system of concepts will be useful in enhancing your perspective. Ideas have a relationship to a big picture context. Concepts interact with other ideas, as gears in machinery. You can study how concepts interact with each other, their classification, diversity, quantity, and competition amongst other ideas. Ideas spawn projects, inventions, and products.

A system is a set of interdependent connected components forming an integrated complex whole. A system is composed of subsystems, and components. It has a structure and culminates in a purpose and function. A system has a boundary and environment that it operates in. All systems have a structure that contains its parts. A system has a behavior, a process, to achieve its purpose or function. The parts are interconnected and have structural or behavioral relationships. A system has subsystems that are composed of elementary parts and process steps.

FRAMEWORK – A framework is a basic structure underlying a system, concept or idea. A conceptual framework is the essential skeleton, or infrastructure for a system. The framework provides a basis for understanding a whole system.

One example of a framework is the science of taxonomy. Taxonomy is the classification of plants and animals according to shared traits, and features. It uses the general principles of scientific classification. The entire science of taxonomy is devoted to looking for overarching principles, features, traits, characteristics, and behaviors that tie together groups of animals and plants. To apply the framework principle, instead of collecting plants and animals, you are looking for a broad, general principle that can bring together all your main ideas.

A proper framework can play a vital role in problem solving and the study of a subject. It creates a foundation upon which all your other work is based upon. A framework will also influence the way you perceive incoming information because try will try to fit it into the mental framework. A properly constructed conceptual framework can also greatly enhance your ability to process information and improve mental fluency. The reason for this is because you can quickly see how a new piece of information fits into the overall schema. In the taxonomy example, when a scientist discovers a new plant or animal, they can quickly classify it based on the taxonomy framework.

PLANNING – Planning is the act of creating a procedure to achieve an objective. It is the art of turning ideas into reality. Planning requires the orchestration of resources, people, information, schedules, budgets, and decisions. Planning is where theory becomes reality. Developing a plan is only possible by comprehending the big picture because it requires seeing how remote parts of a project need to come together. The successful execution of a plan creates outcomes. Planning is an important executive function of the brain.

Planning is a Water thinking principle because it fosters synthesis thinking. Planning requires a big picture view of what you are trying to accomplish. Planning is where lofty goals meets practical implementation. Success incorporates the players into the moving parts of a plan. Planning requires organization, foresight, and anticipation. Plans use coordinated action through synthesis thinking. Water thinking integrates people, resources, ideas together with the big picture.

The kind of thinking required to devise a strategy or plan epitomizes Water thinking. A plan is a procedure to achieve an objective. Planning requires logical thinking, and a procedural sense of how to accomplish an objective. A planner needs to investigate the situation, understand the environment, and know the players involved. It requires a view of the big picture. Synthesis thinking is engaged in developing a plan because you need to see how different parts of a project come together to achieve an objective.

A strategy is the art of devising or employing plans towards a goal (Webster's New World Dictionary, 1984). A plan is created by seeing the big picture and making important associations. The development of a strategy gives you an idea of how to proceed. Once you see big features of the landscape, you can navigate the terrain. Like a roadmap, Water thinking helps you route a path. Air thinking generates creative proposals. The planning principle creates the steps necessary to implement the proposal. Planning gets you to consider the prerequisites necessary to implement a plan of action. Prerequisites can take the form of knowledge, people, resources, skills, and time constraints. Strategies consider how plans fit into a big picture. Plans are used to create a step-by-step roadmap to get you to your objective.

A plan requires the following six elements. First, a plan requires a clear objective to be described. Next, plans need to have S.M.A.R.T. objectives (specific, measurable, achievable, relevant, and time bound). Third, a plan requires a good understanding of the players, the stakeholders, or the groups involved. Fourth, a plan requires the ability to see the intermediate steps necessary to achieve the objective. A plan requires a time-line to be defined. These deadlines specify when tasks need to be accomplished so that they can be coordinated. Finally, the steps of plan need to be communicated to the participants involved.

Objectives – Planning starts with understanding the charter, goals, requirements, and scope that the plan is trying to achieve. The more clearly the objectives can be elucidated the more effective the planning will be. Successful outcomes begin with a clear goal. Good planning requires an understanding of the possible outcomes against the risks, resources, and time constraints.

S.M.A.R.T. objectives – S.M.A.R.T. stands for specific, measurable, achievable, relevant, and time bound. Use S.M.A.R.T. objectives to help identify intermediate progressive steps required to achieve your goal. Reasonable bite-sized steps in planning will make a daunting task less intimidating.

Players – Planning requires a good understanding of the important players involved. You need to identify the key people. Who has the knowledge? Who has the funding? Who has the resources? Planning will often require convincing people with vested interests to share in the vision. Planning requires the collaboration and coordination of the people involved in the project. Communicate who is doing what; and what deliverables they will produce.

Intermediate Steps – Decomposing a large task into a series of progressive steps lies at the heart of planning. Successful planning entails identifying steps to accomplish a larger goal. Break down a complex task into a manageable series of tasks. A large project can be broken down by timelines, subsystems, groups, resources, and deliveries.

Timeline – Planning requires understanding the timelines involved. When do certain resources become available? How long will parts of the project take to finish? How long will it take to accomplish each of the various steps that need to come together? Coordinating each of these steps requires a good understanding of the timelines that it takes to finish each of these steps. Successful coordination of timelines produces successful outcomes in the project.

Communication – Clearly communicating the plan to all the players involved is crucial to success. Coordinating a group of people or coordinating your own activities requires that you clearly express your plans, the objectives, the steps, and the timeline.

Plans can be developed for simple and complex tasks. They can be used in life-long goals and planning daily activities. By planning everyday activities, you will develop the skills needed to devise more grand plans. The perspective component is practiced through the creation of plans.

VIEWPOINT – A viewpoint is a position from which something is observed, it is an attitude or way of considering a matter. Viewpoints can create reality filters and belief structures that change how we see the world. A different or unique viewpoint is at the very heart of the perspective component of Water thinking. Being able to think of a problem from different vantage points, different angles, from different people's perspectives is the main objective of the perspective component.

To see things from a different view point you may need to get yourself to break your conditioning, mental shackles, and step outside of your comfort zone. Take an interest in the subject matter from a different point of view. Describe a problem or subject to another person as see how they would approach the problem differently than you would. Study deeply and broadly so that you may learn how others have considered your subject matter. Take an interest in the experiences of others. Talking to experts is a good way to learn the insights that they have gained. Seeing how other people approach a problem, learning from experts, and considering radical opinions will open your mind to new points of view.

The willingness to look at a situation from a different viewpoint is half the battle. The deliberate, conscious effort to see the world from a different vantage point will often yield results. There are many ways that you might consider a subject from a different perspective. You might be able to physically consider the subject from different geographical locations, angles, or vantage points. You might be able to think of conceptual subject viewed from different disciplines: scientific, psychological, engineering, medicine, ethical, philosophical. The subject might be looked at considering social, moral, ethical, political, financial, institutional, governmental, and international viewpoints. The point is that if you try, you will often be able to think of a subject from many different points of view. In so doing, you will open new mental doors which may lead you down new avenues of thinking that you would have otherwise missed.

WATER THINKING – PERSPECTIVE		
WATER COMPONENT	**PRINCIPLE**	**DESCRIPTION**
PERSPECTIVE	Big Picture & Maps	The big picture is a diagrammatic representation of a concept showing relevant major features. A map is a diagrammatic representation of a geographical area or a conceptual system. The principle of the big picture involves understanding the greater context of a problem or subject. The objective is to understand the greater environment upon which elements of your problem are nestled within.
	Ecology & System	The ecology is the relationship of things and their environment. The mental ecology is a system of concepts and their associated context. A system is a set of interdependent connected components forming an integrated complex whole.
	Framework	A basic structure underlying a system, concept or idea. A conceptual framework is the essential supporting skeleton, scaffolding, infrastructure, and chassis for a system. The framework provides a basis for understanding a whole system.
	Planning	Planning is the act of creating a procedure to achieve an objective. Planning is turning ideas into reality. It orchestrates resources, people, information, schedules, budgets, and decisions. Developing a plan is only possible by comprehending the big picture, and conceptual framework.
	Viewpoint	A viewpoint is a position from which something is observed, it is an attitude or way of considering a matter. Viewpoints can create reality filters and belief structures that change how we see the world.

Table 20 - Water thinking Perspective component principles

Chapter 16 – Water Thinking and Synthesis

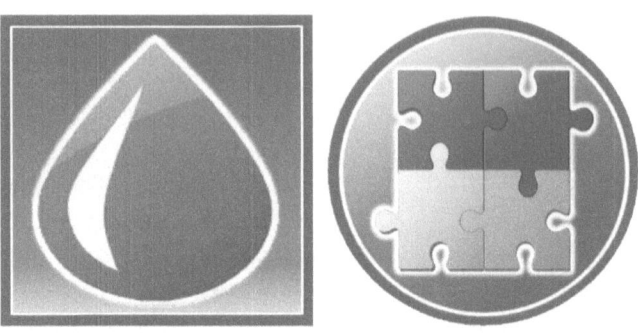

Synthesis is at the heart of water thinking. The objective of the synthesis component is to find ways to merge and join ideas to pave new thinking pathways.

COMPARE & CONTRAST – The human mind thrives on comparisons. Without trying we find familiar patterns for new experiences and things that we encounter. We identify similarities and dissimilarities between things through comparing and contrasting. As a result, our mind connects new ideas in a way that allows us to make sense of our world. If we were unable to see these connections, our thoughts would be incoherent. We would have ideas, but each idea would be isolated. We would be blind as to how new things we encountered related to each other.

Comparison is the one of the methods our brains use to create generalizations, process perceptions, produce concepts, and employ a language. The brain uses comparisons to recognize objects, sounds, tastes, faces, patterns and ideas. We use language to label the familiar objects we come across. If every object we came across could not be compared to existing objects, we would be overwhelmed by our senses. We compare new experiences to existing concepts.

You can see an example of the use of comparing and contrasting. The description of smells and tastes often use comparisons. The smell of a rose might be described using adjectives such as sweet or fragrant. But it can also be described using comparisons to other flowers. The taste of oranges can be reported as juicy, tart, and sweet. But, if you come across a new variety of orange that is a cross-between a grapefruit and an orange, you could describe it by comparing or contrasting it with the qualities of both oranges and grapefruits. A tangelo is a fruit hybrid between a Duncan grapefruit and a Dancy tangerine orange. It is also sometimes referred to as a Honeybell.

If you carefully study your chosen subject matter, comparisons will jump out at you. Many of these will be implicit relationships that we take for granted. Your first goal is to find the characteristics that could serve as a basis for comparison. After that, it is a matter of analysis and thought to see how those qualities relate, differ, contradict, oppose, and synergize with each other.

Contrasting two things requires thought and analysis. To contrast two or more things, you are looking for how those things differ from each other. You want to identify characteristics or aspects of those things make them different. You can try some mental exercises by choosing any two things (for example a cat and a dog) and see if you can compare and contrast them. List all their key identifying characteristics and see how and why they are similar and different. This simple exercise performed with regularity will sharpen your skills. Researchers and scientists use this technique to compare and contrast their work against the existing body of human knowledge. When inventors patent a new idea, they must be aware of existing products and concepts.

CONCLUSION & SUMMARY – A summary is an account of the main points of a concept or idea (Webster's New World Dictionary, 1984). The evidence component of Earth thinking, and the investigation component of Air thinking have coaxed you to gather information and study carefully your chosen subject matter. Water thinking needs to take that jumble of data and find meaningful patterns and connections. These links are the basis of synthesis thinking. One powerful method to help sort through information is to create a summary of what you know. You may also be able to locate summaries that have been produced by others in the subject of interest.

A summary is produced by concisely listing the main points of interest. Those major concepts will each have important sub-points. You can also take all the information that you have available to you and categorize them in some way. You can place events on a timeline. You can place people or things by location. You can sort values numerically. Concepts can be placed in a knowledge tree.

A conclusion is a judgment or decision reached by reasoning. Summaries and conclusions assist in synthesis thinking because of the analysis and thinking that is required. The act of trying to summarize information and evidence will encourage your brain to find important connections between ideas. It will identify the central pillars that are at the heart of your investigations. Once you have these key ideas and central concepts, you will see how things pivot about them. A big picture view, the broader context, environment, and scope of the subject can be understood.

PERMUTATION & COMBINATION – A *combination* is a merging of different parts or qualities where the component elements are individually distinct. A permutation is one of several possible variations, in which a set of things can be ordered or arranged. The permutation is the act of changing the arrangement. Together permutations and combinations can produce variety. The objective of synthesis thinking is to see how things can be combined or related to each other. Diversity can be discovered through combination and permutation.

There are only five basic tastes (salty, sweet, sour, bitter, and umami). But when combined, they give rise to an endless combination of tastes. Computers use ones and zeros to represent data using a binary counting system. There are but seven primary colors (red, orange, yellow, green, blue, indigo, and violet) and yet they produce a medley of colors when blended together. The possible number of patterns that the 100 billion neurons of your brain can make through combination and permutation is more than the number of atoms in the observable universe (Hawkings & Blakeslee, 2005). The combination of elements produces an endless array of molecules. The permutation and combination of elements gives rise to chemistry. The combination of DNA and genes produces a myriad of variety in living organisms (Urry, Cain, Wasserman, & Minorsky, 2016). Basic elements in different permutations and combinations can create a wide variety of results.

The idea is to consider key permutations to stimulate thinking. You can take two concepts and see if they can be bonded together. You can "handshake" two ideas together and see if there is a meaningful combination. You can alter the arrangement of several things and see if that produces something useful. One way to handshake ideas is to use the standard journalistic questions: Who? What? Where? When? Why? and How? Can these two ideas be related by any of those questions? If so, note the association. Sometimes, you will uncover an association you did not consider. You can take the central ideas that you identified by making a summary and see if they can be combined or permutated to stimulate synthesis thinking. Handshaking ideas will get you to think about the elemental aspects of those concepts to see how they might be combined in a new way (Barabasi, 2014).

The concept of combinations and permutations can be used in wide variety of everyday applications. You can use combinations and permutations in getting dressed in the morning. A chef will see culinary possibilities by combining different spices and sauces with different ingredients. You can use combination and permutation in preparing a meal. Permutations and combinations are a developed discipline in mathematics.

THESIS & ANTITHESIS – A thesis is a statement or theory that is put forward as a premise to be proved. An antithesis is a negation or contradiction of the thesis. The synthesis is an analysis of a thesis and antithesis to produce a resolution of the conflict between thesis and antithesis.

A thesis is used to make a conjecture about an issue. Then, an antithesis takes the opposing viewpoint. A synthesis is the resolution between thesis and antithesis. In your personal life, a thesis might be a problem that needs to be solved. The antithesis would be the situation if the problem is not resolved. And the synthesis might be a middle ground between the two.

One approach to Water thinking is the synthesis between a thesis and an antithesis. You can frame any problem large or small in terms of a thesis and antithesis. If you are tackling a problem, you can develop a thesis by expressing it in terms of a hypothesis. A hypothesis is a supposition or proposed explanation made based on limited evidence as a starting point for further investigation.

Researchers and scientists use this powerful concept to frame an issue. The thesis serves as the basis of a hypothesis, and the antithesis is the opposite of that hypothesis. Researchers can take a hypothesis and describe it in statistical terms as the percentage chance that the hypothesis is true. Evidence and experiments are gathered and conducted in search of the truth. Science is progressed through a series of thesis, antithesis and synthesis. A confidence level can be computed between a control group and a treatment group (Trochim, 2001).

TRADEOFFS & COMPROMISE – A trade-off is a balance achieved between two desirable but incompatible features. One quality may be favored over another based on the requirements and objectives of the system. Trade-offs can play a vital role in synthesis thinking because understanding trade-offs allows you to better understand a relationship between two things. A compromise is a settlement or agreement of a dispute that is reached by each side making concessions.

People commonly make trade-offs in everyday life. You have only 24 hours in a day and you must decide what activities that you wish to participate in. You must choose one activity over another favoring one set of values over another. You have only so many resources at your disposal, and you need to make trade-offs of how to spend your money. Maney claimed that a common trade-off is between fidelity (quality) and convenience (Maney, 2010). You have only so much space to live in, and you must decide how you will accommodate your belongings. You must make decisions of what to own and what not to own based on your available living space. Decisions you make about trade-offs in your career, time, space, energy, finances, retirement, personal matters, money, life-work balance, family-career all influence how successful you are in navigating through life.

It is important to be able to recognize a trade-off to incorporate it in your analysis. A trade-off is characterized by a choice. There is some important factor in a decision-making process. They are involved in parameters that can optimize a solution. Trade-offs can exist where alternatives are available. Selecting between two alternatives should immediately signal the presence of trade-offs. Creating alternatives, looking for different possibilities will produce trade-offs that might ultimately lead to a better solution or new ideas.

Compromise is reached by finding a suitable middle ground between the two extremes. A compromise is reached through a deliberate choice. It is a willingness to search for a middle ground, the belief that a solution can be reached where there appears at first to be no solution. The essence of synthesis thinking is the willingness to look for a way which can combine the ideas, proposals, and values to reach an agreeable solution. Often, a problem will have many possible solutions based on trade-offs that are made. One solution may favor one aspect of a trade-off over another. Reaching a compromise requires skill, negotiation, analysis, experience, and balancing trade-offs. You may have to consider agendas, agreements, constraints, finances, people, rules, resources, responsibilities, and values when arriving at a compromise.

In summary, synthesis thinking is the search for new ideas and alternatives through the blending of two other things. The synthesis of two things is an important component of Water thinking. Synthesis thinking involves paving new alternatives and new avenues of thought through combining ideas. Comparing and contrasting allows you to identify similarities and differences. Conclusions and summaries help you develop a bigger picture view. They help you understand the intricate links involved finding a synthesis. Permutations and combinations is one approach in discovering a new synthesis. The identification of a thesis and antithesis are efficient ways to arrive at a synthesis. Identifying and considering tradeoffs helps you reach a compromise which is a form of synthesis.

WATER THINKING – SYNTHESIS		
WATER COMPONENT	**PRINCIPLE**	**DESCRIPTION**
SYNTHESIS	Compare & Contrast	A comparison is a study of differences or similarities between two things. To contrast or juxtapose is to identify distinctive qualities and differences between two things.
	Conclusion & Summary	A summary is an account of the main points of a concept or idea. A conclusion is a judgment or decision reached by reasoning. Summaries and conclusions produce a synthesis through analysis and thinking.
	Permutation & Combination	A combination is a joining or merging of different parts where the component elements were individually distinct. A permutation is one of several possible variations, in which a set or number of things are ordered or arranged. The permutation is the act of changing the arrangement.
	Thesis & Antithesis	A thesis is a statement or theory that is put forward as a premise to be proved. An antithesis is a thing that is the direct opposite of the thesis. An analysis of a thesis and antithesis can generate a synthesis.
	Tradeoffs & Compromise	A trade-off is a balance achieved between two desirable but incompatible features. One quality may be favored based on the requirements and objectives of the system. A compromise is a settlement or agreement of a dispute that is reached by each side making concessions.

Table 21 - Water thinking Synthesis component principles

Chapter 17 – Water Thinking and Pivots

A pivot is an important or central point in a system about which other things revolve around. The identification of a pivot can be instrumental in finding a synthesis between two ideas. A pivot can be a significant point in time that marks a momentous and important change in something. They are moments of commencement, graduation, and ceremony. Pivots are often history-making, such as the discovery of DNA or the invention of the light bulb. Mapping out pivots in the history of something can greatly improve your understanding. Pivotal ideas initiate a domino of events with repercussions that echo through time (Gladwell, 2002). The actions and ideas of some people create important watershed moments.

ANCHOR – A conceptual anchor is a central idea, or thing which serves as a reference point or foundational concept. Concept anchors are the basis from which other ideas revolve. Identifying anchors in a subject matter helps you find key ideas for a subject matter. It will help establish the mental scaffolding to understand a subject of interest. Finding the anchors will help you outline the skeleton from which everything else connects to.

An anchor for a boat is used to fix it to a certain point on the sea. It provides stability. Vessels often need to stay in a stationed position on water when the engines are turned off. The anchor is cast into the sea so that it does not drift from its position due to water currents. An anchor can be used to plant a boat of any size to a reference point at sea. Just as a boat anchor moors a ship to a location in the water, a concept anchor serves as a mental point of reference for a subject. The anchor serves as a means by which the ship can be located at a specific point. A mental anchor serves a similar function. It places a few central ideas or concepts and places them in a specific point in your mind. The anchor places the concept at a central location, known and fixed in your mind. An anchor serves as a mental point of reference. An anchor is a north star, a point to guide by. It is a known point in mental space, and luminous point, a guiding light.

A conceptual anchor is a mental hub, a central focus point. Identifying central ideas is the key to a productive analysis. Some concepts are peripheral, and others play a more important role. Differentiating between the central ideas and peripheral ideas identifies conceptual anchors. Subjects of study and problems are always composed of concepts, ideas, people, events, things, processes, and theories. These things come together to form a conceptual whole, a system. Anchors can be identified by spotting those ideas and things that play an important role in the operation, and conceptualization of something. You are trying to identify the key players, the people who have made a significant contribution. They may be leaders, researchers, experts, or advisors. Anchor concepts are pivots.

One good way to find anchors is to look for patterns in the data. The human mind thrives on patterns. Are there cycles or repetitions in your data? Is there an unusual outstanding event that ties other events together? Is there some common behavior that is displayed? Are there any trends that you can identify? What things are shared by numerous other elements in your problem? Is there some shared feature, or visual cue? Is there some common property or shared trait? Does the data indicate anything being saturated? Can you identify anything that is periodic or seasonal? Are there long-term repetitions or short-term patterns? Are there daily patterns that occur? What might cause these cycles? What factors might cause patterns to be thrown into incoherent chaos? What things have, or might disrupt the patterns? Good thinkers will use a combination of judgment, analysis, and experience identify patterns. What impact will the pattern have for my problem? Why is this pattern relevant? Can you identify any variations of patterns you have already found?

Anchors also play a pivotal role in the future. When the president of a company makes a business decision, it affects hundreds or thousands of people. The president of a country elucidates a vision and steers the efforts of a national economy. Civic leaders are social hubs and serve as an anchor for a community. The leader of a research lab guides the innovative process. Leaders inspire, guide, and steer the development and evolution of ideas and products. Mathematical and scientific laws can predict the behavior of a system. Equations are an example of an anchor in a science.

BOTTLENECK – A bottleneck is a point of congestion or blockage. Conceptually, it is the point in a system or process where many other parts must pass through. Bottlenecks are often where pivots occur because all the elements of a system must pass through that point.

Identifying bottlenecks, points of congestion, limits, and rate limiting factors will help you find the pivots in your system of interest. Bottlenecks can be pivots. They are instrumental because improvements applied to bottlenecks give you disproportionate gains compared to the resources spent.

A bottleneck can be visualized as the long slender neck of a glass bottle. The liquid inside the bottle must flow through the funnel of the neck. It is designed to limit the rate of flow of the liquid from the main reservoir of the bottle. The spout of a tea pot uses the same idea. The design is intention to restrict how much liquid flows out of the container such that the flow of the liquid can be controlled when poured.

Nearly all systems have some sort of bottleneck. Processes all have some restrictive point. Project schedules have a point that other teams depend upon. The project cannot advance without the product of that other team. Traffic flows often have some point of congestion. Checkpoints are bottlenecks since the elements flowing through the system are inspected before being allowed to pass onto the rest of the system. Highway toll booths are an example of a bottleneck since each vehicle must be processed before they can proceed.

Understanding bottlenecks grants insight into the operation of a system. It helps you understand the flow of elements through a system. Identifying bottlenecks will help you find those critical interconnections between subsystems within the greater system. When optimizing a system, it is vital to find these bottlenecks.

I did my Ph.D. in operations research. It is study of optimizing systems (Winston, 1994). To optimize a system, you need to be able to understand and characterize a system. You need to understand the flows and bottlenecks. You need to understand where and how elements arrive and move through a system. By understanding the bottlenecks, you can optimize performance.

CATALYST – A catalyst is something that precipitates an event. It is a concept or idea which facilitates the completion of a project. Catalysts can play a pivotal role in the development of a system. As agents of change, they can help you identify where synthesis can occur within a system.

The chemical definition of a catalyst is a substance that speeds up a chemical reaction but is not consumed or altered in the process (Tro, 2016). A catalyst facilitates the emergence of a pivot. A catalyst is also something that causes activity between two or more persons or forces without itself being affected. It is a person or thing that precipitates an event or change.

Catalysts are vital in chemistry and biology. All enzymes are catalysts that expedite the biochemical reactions necessary for life (Urry, Cain, Wasserman, & Minorsky, 2016). In chemistry, a catalyst is a chemical that makes another chemical reaction take place (Tro, 2016).

It is important to be able to identify a catalyst because it can help you see a synthesis between two things. A catalyst can often play a pivotal role in the change or evolution of something. As such, understanding where and when a major change in a system will occur can help you understand that system better. Water thinking is synthesis thinking, which involves seeing important connections. A pivot is a significant point in time that marks a momentous change. As agents of change in a system, catalysts are often pivots.

An example of a catalyst is the agent, or interface that gets things done. The middleman in a transaction is a catalyst. The internet has replaced many of the traditional catalysts. Buyers can use a retailer's web interface to buy directly from the producer. Real estate agents, travel agents, and stock brokers have been traditional middlemen. Electronic middlemen will be a virtual catalyst to facilitate any transaction. Any transaction can have a catalyst to broker the exchange.

TIPPING POINT – The tipping point is a point where dramatic change happens in a system. An example of the tipping point is when an idea is suddenly accepted by most people in a population. The term *"going viral"* is used to describe an idea that has reached a tipping point to "infect" the minds of the general populous.

A book called *"The Tipping Point"* by Malcolm Gladwell describes a set of circumstances where an idea or product propagates through a large portion of society attaining high levels of popularity (Gladwell, 2002). Today, this phenomenon is called "going viral", named after a condition with a virus that spreads and replicates quickly throughout cells. Gladwell claims that there are three main mechanisms that create tipping points. The first one he calls "the law of the few" whereby a small number of socially gifted individuals help to spread an idea. The second is *"the stickiness factor"* which is defined as the elements of an idea that makes it memorable thereby enhancing its ability to attract more aficionados. Lastly, the "*power of context*" described environmental factors that help to promote an idea.

The tipping point is a pivot because it is the source of widespread change. Understanding how an idea can propagate quickly and pervasively is important for ideas, products, public policy, cultural customs, art, and marketing campaigns. Tipping points become pivotal when they reach a broad audience. The mechanisms to achieve a tipping point are useful to understand. These mechanisms can often determine the success or failure of a product. They can determine the popularity of a cultural icon. Understanding how an idea spreads throughout a population will influence how an idea should be promoted, communicated, and developed.

Suppose you could foresee tipping points. You would be able to predict negotiation outcomes, conflict resolutions, cresting stock markets, bursting investment bubbles, emerging fashion trends, blossoming artists, gripping must-have holiday products, influential discoveries, transformative inventions, popular retail products, and booming markets. These examples illustrate that tipping points are pivotal because their impact echoes throughout society. Pivotal products bring widespread changes and sometimes create revolutions within their industry. Ideas reach a tipping point when they come to grip many minds. Financial markets reach a pivot through a boom or bust.

TREND – A trend is a general direction of observable outcomes from a system. It is a broad tendency of beliefs held by many people, or a consensus. It is what happens when many people participate in an activity or believe in a notion. A trend can also be a general direction of change or development. A trend is also a set of beliefs held by many people, or a consensus.

Trends tend to be a central focus of social attention. After a pivotal event has occurred, a trend may be created. It is insightful to identify trends in data. Are there common observable behaviors or beliefs held by a large group of people? Trends can help you anticipate an outcome because it can indicate a direction or tendency towards an objective or subject.

A significant portion of the population that dresses a certain way is a fashion trend. Popular sports can create sporting trends particularly around the time of championships. Some examples include the soccer world cup, Olympics, Tennis world championships. Political trends can cause a viewpoint to come into or out of favor. Media trends are the result of the general populous fixating upon a specific work. Social media websites such as twitter and Facebook are examples of social trends. Every country has food trends where certain foods or drinks become popular. Exercise trends come into favor when a significant portion of the population engages in it. Trends are important because they can cause organizations, companies, and people to spring into action and rally behind those people pursuing that trend.

No matter the objective of your thinking journeys, spotting trends can help you see the broader picture, understand the context of events, and influence your exploration of a subject. Trends can influence your personal life from a social standpoint, to a financial one. Trends affect many aspects of our lives. They can influence the people we associate with socially. Trends can affect what things we buy and invest our time in. Trends impact our decisions, who we befriend, and what causes we devote our lives to. Trends may help define what things are meaningful to us.

In summary, Pivots are an important or central point around which other things revolve. The Pivots component has anchor, bottlenecks, tipping point, and trends as principle ideas. The identification of a pivot can be instrumental in finding a synthesis between two ideas. A pivot can be a significant point in time that marks a momentous and important change in something. Commencements, inaugurations, graduations, and ceremonies are public events that socially acknowledge a pivotal event. Mapping out pivots can improve your understanding of your chosen subject. Pivotal ideas initiate a domino of events with repercussions that echo through time. Anchors serves a point of reference or a foundation upon which to build from. Bottlenecks are points of congestion or pivotal points in a process where many things flow through. Understanding bottlenecks can be the key to unlocking the full potential of a process, system, or idea. A catalyst is a facilitator that assists in the completion of a process, or event. Identifying the catalysts can be instrumental in the completion of projects. The Tipping Point is a point where dramatic changes can occur. A tipping point occurs when the behavior of a system changes from one mode of to another. Trends mark a general change in direction or observable behavior by a large group of people. Trends can help you predict outcomes and prepare for the future. Trends can help you see the points of synthesis between people and ideas, places and products, money flows and markets, groups and functions.

WATER THINKING – PIVOTS		
WATER COMPONENT	**PRINCIPLE**	**DESCRIPTION**
PIVOTS	Anchor	A conceptual anchor is a central idea, or thing which serves as a reference point or foundation concept. Concept anchors are the basis from which other ideas revolve.
	Bottlenecks	A bottleneck is a point of congestion or blockage. It is the point in a system or process where many other parts must pass through. For example, in a chemical reaction, it is rate-limiting factor. Bottlenecks are often where pivots occur.
	Catalyst	A catalyst is something that precipitates an event. It is a concept or idea which facilitates the completion or progress of a project. A catalyst facilitates the emergence of a pivot.
	Tipping Point	The tipping point is a point where dramatic change happens in a system. For example, when an idea is suddenly accepted by most people in a population. An idea goes viral by reaching a tipping point to "infect" the minds of many. The tipping point is a pivot.
	Trend	A trend is a general direction of observable outcomes from a system. A broad tendency of beliefs held by many people, or a consensus. A central focus of social attention for a time. After a pivotal event has occurred, a trend is created.

Table 22 - Water thinking Pivots component principles

Chapter 18 –Fire Thinking and Decisions

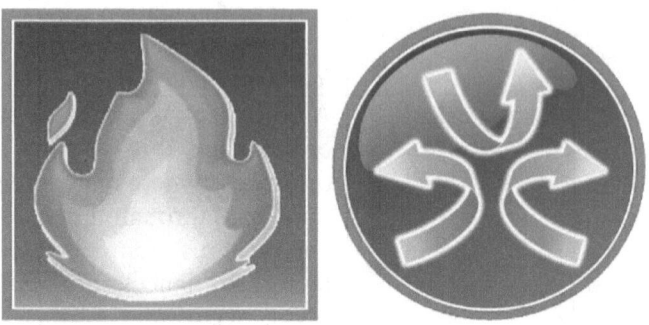

The first component of Fire thinking is decisions. We all make choices; but, in the end, our choices make us. You are a product of the choices you have made in life. Learning how to make good decisions is the foundation for a productive, happy, and successful life. Decisions can steer us in a direction that aligns with our goals and objectives. Bad decisions can take us down the wrong path. The decisions we make in life echo down your history.

The decisions component is comprised to the following principles: *goals*, *constraints*, *alternatives*, *criteria*, *consequences*, and *selection*. Together, these principles will step you through the decision-making process to make intelligent, informed and wise decisions. Each of these decision-making aspects are explored:

GOALS - Consider the perfect solution to the problem. Because tradeoffs must be made in decision-making, no proposal will be truly perfect. First, consider the "best of all worlds". The idea is to get insight into what factors are critical. The goal is to define what an ideal solution would be. Try to identify the ideal solution. Try to specify details about the ideal solution. Decisions are based, in part, on your preferences. Defining a goal gives you a target to aim for, and it creates a metric by which you can judge proposals against.

Once you have defined an objective, determining which of your proposals is closest to the ideal goal will be much easier. By specifying an ideal solution, you will be able to gain insight into your preferences, and objectives. Defining a goal allows you to gauge how close each of your alternatives is to your ideal specification. You can ascertain what qualities of each alternative made it close to the ideal. Defining a goal will allow you to consider what aspects could be altered to make the proposal match closer to the ideal. When defining a goal, it may help to first make a list of important qualities of your ideal solution.

Defining a goal for your decision-making process should help guide your decisions, provide clarity, create standards to measure choices against, help identify important decision factors, and increase motivation to find a choice. When defining goals, you can consider the decision from different aspects.

CONSTRAINTS – When making decisions, you need to take into consideration the *constraints* and *requirements*. Decisions will have certain constraints that your decision must adhere to. Constraints might eliminate certain decision choices or favor a specific alternative. There might be limits to the amount of resources, or knowledge that need to be considered during the decision-making process. A requirement is a necessary condition that your decision must satisfy.

A constraint will influence what alternatives are viable. Constraints will dictate if certain people need to be selected, if specific things must be considered, or the solution must be in a certain place.

ALTERNATIVES – Alternatives represents the choices from which to make selections from. In the decision-making process, you are always choosing between multiple alternatives. What makes decisions difficult is that you are giving up certain potential outcomes and favor of other ones. *Decision regret* occurs when you have anxiety about unexplored possibilities might have been a better choice.

Identifying alternatives are part and parcel to making wise, intelligent and efficient decisions. The sooner you can identify all the viable alternatives, the better the potential outcomes. Alternatives are a set of proposals that are offered to resolve a problem. Suppose, you want to renovate your home and you would like to contract out the work. Your alternatives might be the three different contractors with the expertise necessary to complete the renovation project you have in mind.

The alternatives must obey the constraints, and often you will discover that multiple alternatives will often accomplish (or come close to accomplishing) your goals. The first step towards good decision-making is to identify the possible alternatives that might accomplish your goal. Differentiating between the optimal but difficult versus the easy but sub-optimal ones is akin to finding the best path through the forest. Some choices set before you will represent a difficult path but with rewarding possibilities. Others will be easy paths to take but may have undesirable consequences. Yet, other choices will fall somewhere in between those two extremes. Risk and reward, constraints and restrictions, goals and objectives, tradeoffs and compromises are the factors which will determine which alternatives are viable.

CRITERIA – Criteria are the factors used in decision-making. These are the qualities by which you will judge if one alternative is better than another one. Once you have defined your criteria, they will become the standard, metric, and yardstick to gauge one alternative versus another.

Criteria are relevant factors to consider in the decision-making process. The more criteria you are considering the longer the decision will take to make, but the more carefully considered your decision will have been. Important capital decisions or life-altering decisions should garner more attention. Carefully describe the factors that are important.

Some of the questions to consider which may lead you to discover important criteria are: Who should also be involved? Who has a stake in the decision-making process? Who does this decision impact? Who is trying to influence the decision? Who has a vested interest in the problem? Who might be helped or harmed? What are the most important factors to consider? What is the environment or surroundings related to the problem? What background do you need to learn? What is the context of the decision? What will be the long-term consequence of this decision? What opportunity will be lost or created by this decision? What is applying pressure to decide? What are the alternatives? What is the worst outcome of a bad decision? What is the benefit of making a good decision? What happens if no decision is made? What are the desirable qualities you are looking for? What are the risks? What are the rewards? What extenuating circumstances are there? What physical factors are important to think about? What financial considerations are there? What would a satisfying outcome be? What vested interest do you have in the problem? What factors did other people consider when making a similar decision? What resources are necessary to consider? What geographical factors are important to consider? What permanence does the decision have? What would cause you to reject an alternative outright? What things matter to you the most? What things matter to you the least? What would it take to implement the decision? Why is it important to decide? When does the decision need to be made by? When will the consequences of the decision be apparent? Where will the decision be made? Where are the important locations to consider? How many people should be involved in the decision-making process? How will you know if a decision is flawed? Could the decision be reversed?

When trying to identify the criteria, you are seeking qualities that may influence the function and form of a solution. How would your alternatives change with different criteria? Criteria should help you choose between outcomes. What qualities would help you select between one alternative over another?

There are several common types of major decisions. These include deciding on: capital purchases, causes to support, schools to attend, your life purpose, vacation destinations, career paths, and family decisions. Major decisions affect your future. The following table captures some typical criteria for these common types of major decisions.

DECISION TYPES	COMMON CRITIERA FOR THESE DECISION TYPES
Purchasing (vehicle, home)	Capabilities, capacity, color, cost, crash test results, ease of use, energy efficiency, function, handling, interior design, manufacturer, previous owners, rarity, reviews, performance, quality, recommendations, size, style, weight
Supporting causes (community)	Alignment to your values & interests, endorsements, opportunity cost, personal value, recommendations, social significance, supporters, time commitment, worthiness
School selection	Accommodations, accreditations, admission rate, amenities, availability, career options, cost, courses offered, curriculum, demographics, facilities, faculty, fees, food facilities, graduation rate, location, quality of institution, quality ratings, retention rate, reviews, school size, social activities, student composition, teacher to student ratio, transportation
Recreation decisions (vacation, hobbies, travel, activities, events, entertainment)	Accommodations, cost, culture, dangers, distance, food, ease of travel, health risks, historical significance, local holidays, location, man-made attractions, native languages, natural attractions, people, personal interest, political conditions, previous experiences, purpose of travel, recommendations, safety concerns, special events, time investment, travel logistics, vicarious experiences, visa requirements
Deciding meaningful life purpose	Appealing virtues, Beliefs, feelings of fulfillment, happiness factors, meaningful experiences, proud moments, personal values,
Career decisions, Job change	Alignment with values, compensation, expectations, experience, industry, impact to personal future, knowledge required, logistics, long-term prospects, networking, obstacles, opinions, organization, personal happiness, qualifications, quality of organization, recommendations, resources, skill set required, staff, timing of change, vested interest, work-life balance
Family decisions (find partners, family decisions)	Beliefs, compatibility, costs, emotional value, interest, life outlook, life priorities, money, personal desires, ready for life change, respect, shortcomings, social pressure, time, trustworthiness, value alignment

Table 23 - Fire thinking decision-making criteria

There will be specialized decisions you have to make. These questions will be helpful: How will a decision be made between these two alternatives? What is important to consider? Why is this decision difficult? What needs to be considered when making this decision? How will it be judged? What factors will likely be incorporated? Why is this decision important? What are the stumbling blocks?

CONSEQUENCES – The consequences describe the worst-case scenarios, and repercussions that can result from a decision. This step of decision-making is a sanity check on the decision-making process. Consequences need to be considered as part of evaluating alternatives against a set of criteria and constraints. Some of the selection methods will describe "what if" scenarios, which are situations that can arise to challenge the successful implementation of a decision. Thinking about worst case scenarios often makes a solution more robust.

Think of your problem, your situation, your environment, the system, the people and objects involved in the solution. What are things that can go wrong? If problems arose what are things that would be useful on hand to help alleviate the problem or mitigate the damage?

It is often useful to consider the repercussions that can result from a decision. How will this decision shoot through time? Will the decision matter tomorrow, next month, or next year? In what way will your future be affected by this decision? You will find it helpful to visualize the repercussions of a decision. This confirms that your decision is in line with your goals and will have the desired impact on the future. Alternatively, it may raise doubts and concerns that need to be addressed. How will this decision affect other people? What are the financial consequences and risks associated with the implementing the decision? Are these repercussions acceptable? Identify the key consequences for consideration in the selection process.

SELECTION – Now that you have identified your goals, constraints, criteria and alternatives you are ready to select. Your goals have defined your objectives and what you are trying to achieve with your decision. The constraints impose requirements that your choices must adhere to. The criteria are factors by which to judge between alternatives. The alternatives are the choices you will be selecting between.

How do you select one of your alternatives? The following table summarizes some of the selection methods that you can use to select between alternatives. Each will be described in more detail.

FIRE THINKING – SELECTION		
FIRE PRINCIPLE	SELECTION METHOD	DESCRIPTION
SELECTION METHOD	Best Fit	The Best fit selection method tries to identify the optimal situation.
	Devil's Advocate	The Devil's Advocate method lists the flaws, negative consequences for each alternative.
	Matrix Method	This method creates a matrix of factors & weights for each alternative. A quantitative method weighing each alternative against a set of selection criteria.
	Feasibility Focus	This method selects the most feasible and viable alternative. It is focused on the ability to execute and implement a solution.

Table 24 - Fire thinking Selection methods

The following selection methods are tools which can be applied to help you select between alternatives.

BEST FIT - The best fit method focuses on finding the optimal situation or context in which a proposal would be ideally suited. This method is particularly useful when the environment, background, context, or circumstance is of principle concern. This decision method tries to determine which alternative most closely matches your ideal situation. This acknowledges that a perfect candidate may not exist; however, consider which of the available options most closely matches your conception of an ideal choice (Lehrer, 2010).

First, for each of your proposed alternatives consider the people, places and things that are associated with them. Next, for each alternative, highlight the criteria and constraints that you identified that are related to the environment, context, or background. Then, consider these criteria and constraints for each of your alternatives. Do any of the alternatives seem to fit the constraints better than the others? Given your criteria, do any of the alternatives stand out? Next, you can identify important factors for each of the environments. Give each of your criteria and constraints more consideration with respect to the environment.

You can also use the best fit method by considering each alternative one at a time and ranking them against the criteria, constraints and goals. These will be your alternatives.

Lastly, consider what is important to you. If this is a personal decision, a best fit solution may be identified by factoring your values. What is important to you in life? Why is this decision important in the big scheme of your life? Values may provide a guiding hand during the decision-making process. Is there a relevant policy or rule that has already been established that can be applied to this decision?

DEVIL'S ADVOCATE – When all the alternatives at hand seem equally appealing, deciding can be tortuously difficult. The difficulty lies in the fact that we must bring ourselves to give up an attractive alternative. You only have so much time and resources to commit to activities. However, in real life, very few things are perfectly equally appealing. The goal is to find some way to differentiate between these alternatives.

In a case where the alternatives seem to be equally appealing, you can try the Devil's Advocate method. Start by listing all the downsides, flaws, negative consequences and problems with each alternative. The Devil's Advocate method scrutinizes each alternative by considering their associated shortcomings. Next, imagine that you are staunchly opposed to each of the proposals. This method deliberately considers the downside because it is often easier to differentiate alternatives this way.

Consider some of the following questions and see if they can help differentiate between alternatives. You can ask: what are the issues with these alternatives? Who would be opposed to the proposals? What vested interests would oppose implementation of these ideas? What could go wrong during implementation? What safety issues exist with these proposals? What are the financial risks and burdens to these proposals? Why would these solutions not work? What groups of people might be excluded? What goals are not being met? What sort of circumstances or environmental problems might cause these solutions to fail? What fail-safes and contingency plans are still needed? What negative long-term consequences are there? Where does this proposal overrun the available resources? What constraints does these proposals violate?

When a decision or proposal is evaluated by a group, you will often find resistance to that idea. There are many methods by which new ideas are challenged. The five most common strategies are: appeal to the status quo, confusion, delay, fear tactics, and ridicule. Other objections that people use are based on the fallacies of thinking which will be described in a later chapter.

When used effectively, the devil's advocate can facilitate making decisions by rejecting the less perfect alternatives. Make a list of answers to the above questions for each proposal and then compare the alternatives against each other. See if one of the alternatives achieves your goals best while still adhering to your constraints. Let the devil's advocate method be an assistant to decision-making. You will often find, as you use this method, that you will start to mentally favor one or two of the alternatives.

Suppose you have a situation where none of the alternatives looks very appealing. You can try a variant method which I will dub the "Angel's Advocate". In this variation, you ask yourself what changes would be necessary for some of the alternatives to be acceptable? Instead of finding flaws to reach a decision, you are doing the reverse, finding strengths to bolster. What qualities would make some of the candidate proposals attractive and viable?

MATRIX METHOD – The decision matrix method for decision selection methodically compares each of the alternatives against the criteria and constraints. This technique was invented by Stuart Pugh (Pugh, 1981); and is also known as the Pugh Concept Selection method. This method considers each alternative and evaluates it against each of the criteria and constraints to determine the best alternative for the decision objective. This is the most analytical method of all the selection techniques because it uses quantitative rankings of the alternatives matched against the relevant decision factors (criteria and constraints).

A matrix is a grid table with rows and columns. Along the left side of the grid (the row titles) you list the alternatives. Then, along the top of the grid (the column headers) you list the relevant criteria and constraints. At the intersection of each row and column represents a specific factor for one specific alternative. This method makes you consider each criteria and constraint against every alternative. You can implement a simpler version of this method by simply placing an "X" instead of a number to indicate that this option satisfies the desired characteristic. Then you add up all the numbers (or "X"'s) across each row. Thus, you will end up with a score for each vehicle. The highest scoring alternative is the best choice. The following table illustrates choosing between three vehicles:

Selection Methods – Matrix Method – Criteria & Constraints

	versus Alternatives				
	Criteria: features	Criteria: performance	Criteria: safety	Constraint: cost	**TOTAL**
Vehicle 1	8	8	8	5	29
Vehicle 2	5	5	9	8	27
Vehicle 3	7	7	9	7	30

Table 25 - Fire thinking selection method - Matrix Method

A more advanced variation of the matrix method is to give each criteria and constraint a different weighting factor. You can give each chosen factor a weight (number) and multiply the weight by the value you gave to a specific choice before adding across the rows. The following table illustrates a use of the weighted matrix method:

	Selection Methods – Matrix Method – Criteria & Constraints versus Alternatives				
	Criteria: features Weight = 1	Criteria: performance Weight = ½	Criteria: safety Weight = 2	Constraint: cost Weight = 2	**TOTAL**
Vehicle 1	8x1 = 8	8x ½ = 4	8 x 2 =16	5 x 2 = 10	38
Vehicle 2	5x1 = 5	5x½ = 2½	9x2 = 18	8x2 = 16	41 ½
Vehicle 3	7x1 = 7	7x½ = 3½	9x2 = 18	7x2 = 14	42 ½

Table 26 - Fire thinking selection method – Weighted matrix method

This method considers some "what if" scenarios when considering a constraint against an alternative. In these situations, you are anticipating situations that might arise. How would your alternative fair in a hypothetical situation?

The key aspect of the matrix method is that it makes you carefully consider all the factors against all the options. Because of its thoroughness, this technique is well suited for major, important decisions. As you can see from the examples above, it is an analytical method that encourages you to quantify critical qualities with respect to criteria and constraints of all your alternatives.

FEASIBILITY FOCUS – The feasibility focus method opts for the most straight-forward, most feasible, and viable proposal to implement. This method is concerned with the ability to implement and execute upon a proposal. The fruition of a decision is of prime importance. This method favors a solution that is feasible, and the one that is most viable to execute. All decisions eventually translate into actions. This method picks an alternative that is most likely to be realized.

You can start thinking about your alternatives from a feasibility standpoint by considering the following questions: How difficult will this proposal be to implement? What steps are needed to implement this proposal? Who needs to be involved with implementation? What skills, knowledge, approvals, resources, finances, tools will need to be acquired before you can start? How long will it take? What roadblocks, opposition and obstacles need to be overcome? What things must come together to produce the final product? How would those things be coordinated? Asking yourself questions related to making these alternatives a reality will help you decide which one is the best from a feasibility standpoint.

Another approach is to assign a "feasibility" score to each of your proposals. Then, you eliminate the most complex and unrealistic alternatives. Is it obvious from the remaining proposals which one is the most feasible one? If so, then adopt the most feasible candidate as your final decision. The objective for this selection method is to favor the alternative that will most likely become a reality. The feasibility focus method is suited to problems where the decision results in implementing a plan.

Next, you can create "what if?" scenarios that stress test your alternatives. This will help you identify your most feasible alternatives. To create these scenarios, suppose that bad things occurred while you were trying to implement your solutions. Keep producing "what if" questions until you have gotten a better understanding of your alternatives. This method indicates which alternatives are the most robust under duress.

Identify which of the "what if" scenarios are the most likely to occur. Pick which what-if scenarios that are the most important ones to you. You can test each choice against each scenario and see which ones fail. Hopefully, the what-if scenarios should help you identify your most feasible solutions. The "what-if" method will give insight into your problem.

Remember that many decisions will not have a perfect choice. Sometimes there will be several equally good choices. You might find yourself in a situation where you would achieve your objectives with any of available choices.

To summarize, your goals have defined your decision objectives. This is what you are trying to achieve with your decision. The constraints impose requirements that your choices must adhere to. The criteria are factors by which to judge between alternatives. The alternatives are the choices you will be selecting between. Thinking about consequences allows you to reflect upon possible worst-case scenarios and repercussions of a decision.

FIRE THINKING – DECISIONS		
FIRE COMPONENT	**PRINCIPLE**	**DESCRIPTION**
DECISIONS	Goals	The goal describes the ideal solution and objectives that a decision is trying to achieve. The goal encompasses the problem statement to be addressed with the decision.
	Constraints	Constraints describe the requirements and restrictions that your final choice or solution must conform to.
	Alternatives	Alternatives are the choices, possibilities and options that a decision will select from.
	Criteria	Criteria are factors that play a role in decision-making. They are principles, measures, standards, or trade-offs that should be considered during decision-making.
	Consequences	The consequences describe the worst-case scenarios, contingencies, and repercussions that can result from a decision
	Selection	Selection is the process of picking between alternatives taking into consideration the goals, constraints, criteria and consequences.

Table 27 - Fire thinking Decision component principles

Chapter 19 –Fire Thinking and Judgment

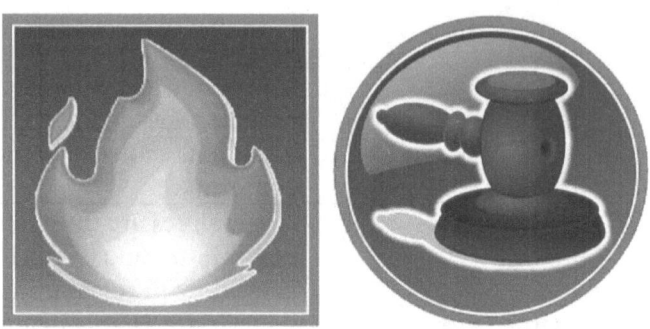

This chapter is about the judgment component of Fire thinking. Judgment plays a vital role in evaluation. Good judgment has five principles: thinking fallacies, experience, objectivity, scrutiny and wisdom. Awareness of the <u>fallacies of thinking</u> allows you to sidestep mental traps thereby honing your evaluative skills. They will be described in the next chapter. <u>Experience</u> is your prior knowledge, skill and history in a subject. It allows you to predict outcomes and avoid pitfalls. Experience develops your intuition on a subject facilitating quick assessments or in-depth analysis. <u>Objectivity</u> allows you to analyze a situation without bias. <u>Scrutiny</u> is the critical assessment and examination of an idea. <u>Wisdom</u> is the ability to apply experience, knowledge and good judgment to actions and decisions. These principles will be used to evaluate and refine proposals and ideas.

SCRUTINY - Scrutiny is defined as the critical assessment of an idea or proposal. You can scrutinize the quality of a solution through its relevancy and efficacy. Wisdom guides your analysis through prudence and common sense.

Using scrutiny, you will evaluate an idea critically. The objective of scrutiny is to find areas for improvement, ways to hone a candidate proposal. Also, you want to acknowledge parts of an idea that are already outstanding as a basis to build upon. The goal is to transform a dysfunctional proposal into a feasible one or make an adequate idea better. The scrutiny principle critically evaluates a proposal by finding weaknesses you have identified areas for improvement. Worst-case scenarios prompt you to create contingency plans. Thoughtful decision-making sets you on the course to success. Breaking a problem down into manageable parts allows you to methodically consider different aspects of the subject matter. Every problem is unique. You should ask yourself "what works?", "what doesn't?" and "what can be done about it?" The objective of scrutiny is to shore up those aspects of an idea that fall short of fulfilling the objectives and requirements of a problem.

Breaking down a proposal makes it more manageable to assess. Break down a problem, and then evaluate the different parts separately. This facilitates analysis because there is less complexity and fewer interactions to consider. This allows you to find incompatible parts in a proposal and gets you to consider how each part impacts the overall solution. After you have broken down a proposal, you can use scrutiny on each of the components.

Flaws are where a proposal falls short of meeting the requirements of a problem. List all the flaws that jump out at you. Consider what scenarios will cause proposal to fail. Then, identify the merits. Understanding merits helps you understand the flaws. Next, think of possible ways to address the flaws.

The decision component selected candidate proposals. The Judgment component of Fire thinking refines solutions, transforming them into feasible solutions. Do not use Fire thinking to merely reject a solution outright. Use evaluation as a basis for wise analysis and to address specific flaws. Improve parts of an idea with the objective of refining the overall proposal. By listing down the flaws with a solution you will be able to stimulate contingency plans.

One of the main obstacles with identifying flaws is vested interest. Once someone has settled on an idea, they have a vested interest in it. It transforms an idea into a belief. As a result, people tend to defend their beliefs against all attack. However, ideas are vulnerable to a variety of errors such as logical errors, inaccurate facts, changing circumstances, imperfections, and flawed analysis.

Another pitfall is becoming too familiar with a problem. The longer you work on a problem, the closer you become to the issues the more accustomed you become to the details. You must mentally distance yourself to objectively evaluate proposals. Identifying flaws with a proposal is a healthy part of good thinking.

Constructive criticism is necessary in problem solving. There is usually room for improvement: circumstances arise, preferences change, the problem statement evolves, and flaws are uncovered. Constructive criticism starts by asking probing questions. This locates imperfections for refinement. By asking the right questions and thinking of challenging scenarios you can anticipate complications. This addresses these scenarios by refining the proposal or developing contingency plans.

Consider the following questions in identifying imperfections:

A. **APPEARANCE** – Is appearance important for your problem or solution? How can the appearance be improved? Are there flaws in the appearance?

B. **CLARITY** – Is the solution difficult to understand? Is it difficult to implement? Is it difficult to communicate to others?

C. **COMPATIBILITY** –Do other things depend on this solution? Is this solution dependent upon something else? Is there a mismatch to be addressed?

D. **COMPETITION** – What are the competing solutions? How is this solution better than others? What disadvantages does this proposal have?

E. **COMPONENTS** – What are the fundamental components of the solution? How were the components chosen? Are some of the components interchangeable?

F. **CONFIGURATION** – What parts of the system mix and match to produce different configurations? Are there other layouts that could have been chosen?

G. **CONSEQUENCES** – What are the implications of the idea? What undesirable consequences will result from this proposal? How could those be overcome?

H. **CONVENIENCE** – How easy is the solution to implement? How easy it is to use? How convenient is it for the users? How can its convenience be improved?

I. **DURABILITY** – How robust is the solution? How dependable is the process? How reliable is the solution? What is the mean time between failures (MTBF)?

J. **ECONOMY** – How costly is the solution to implement? How can the cost be reduced? Is cost an important factor? What are the projected cost expenditures?

K. **EFFICIENCY** – Does the proposed solution efficiently solve the problem? Does a competing solution offer better efficiency?

L. **EMOTION** – Emotions can influence our choices, desires and values. After you explore the problem, consider the emotional factors involved.

M. **ENVIRONMENT** – Are there environmental concerns that impede the efficacy of the solution? What environmental factors need to be considered?

N. **ERGONOMICS** – How easy is it for a person to use this idea? When people interact with the solution, what human factors need to be considered?

O. **EXTRANEOUS ELEMENTS** – Are there things that are unnecessary in the solution? Eliminate things that are complex just for the sake of complexity.

P. **FORM** – What is the form of the solution? The "form" of the solution refers to both the physical shape and conceptual composition of the solution.

Q. **FUNCTION** – How functional is the solution? Function refers to the ability of the solution to meet the requirements of the problem.

R. **HISTORY** – Does history play a role in the solution? If you are dealing with a physical thing, what is the history of it? Are past events important to consider?

S. **OPERATIONAL** – Are there operational flaws? Is the solution difficult to implement? What skills are necessary to operate the solution?

T. **PHYSICAL CONCERNS** – Are there flaws related to the physical aspects of the problem? Are there problems you can identify related to physical attributes?

U. **PRACTICAL** – How practical is the solution? Can its practicality be improved? What makes the solution impractical?

V. **SAFETY** – Under what circumstance would the solution pose a threat to someone? What could break? If something broke, how could it be fixed?

W. **SECURITY** – What are the security concerns? How important is security to the problem? What harm could a malicious person cause?

X. **SIMPLICITY** – Is the solution unnecessarily complex? How can it be simplified? What things might be combined to offer greater simplicity?

Y. **TIME** – Is time a factor? Is the timing of things in the solution important? Does a solution need to be realized in a particular time frame? What

Z. **VALUE** – Is there something physically valuable? What factors alter the value? Has the value been assessed? What economic factors need to be accounted for?

AA. **VESTED INTERESTS** – What groups would be affected by this proposal? Who might be impacted? Are there existing groups that are impacted negatively?

   Thinking about the shortcomings of a proposal encourages you to improve a proposal to address flaws. After you have tackled some of possible pitfalls, you can then consider how the proposed solution will be used. The objective of the scrutiny principle is not just to find flaws but ultimately to make a solution feasible. Thinking about the applications can enhance a solution because you are anticipating how a solution might be used. Listing the possible applications is a valuable exercise because it may suggest ways to improve the design or proposal. Consider the following questions:

A. **COMPLEXITY** – What steps are involved when using the solution? Where are the complexities in the proposal? What components or groups need to be coordinated? How does the complexity influence the applications?

B. **TARGET AUDIENCE** – Who is the intended target audience or user? Who will most likely use your solution? Who would it benefit the most? How will they react this idea? Consider an unintentional user. How might they misuse it?

C. **CONTEXT** – How is the solution best used? Under what context, environment or circumstances is the idea best applied? Does it have a time constraint or timetable? Visualize the setting, location, position, audience related to the idea.

D. **PHYSICAL CONSTRAINTS** – Where is the solution best implemented? Does it have a physical restriction? Are there geographical locations to consider? How might the applications for the proposal vary based on physical constraints?

E. **ECONOMICS** – How much will it cost? Who will finance it? How would cost determine who uses the solution? Is the projected cost of the idea acceptable to the target audience? Are less expensive alternatives already available?

F. **TOOLS** – What tools are required? Will the necessary tools affect how someone might use the solution? Can the tools be built in or packaged with a solution? Could the solution be simplified to require fewer specialized tools?

G. **PREREQUISITES** – What prerequisites does the idea require? What knowledge, skills or other resources are required? Will the prerequisites affect how you might use the idea? Does a user need to learn any new knowledge?

H. **OPERATIONAL CONSIDERATIONS** – Are there operational considerations? How would a user operate the solution? Is a solution befuddling? Where might a user get confused in trying to use, or operate the solution?

I. **REHEARSAL** – Step through in your mind's eye someone using the solution. What stumbling points to you foresee? Where is someone likely to apply the solution in a unique fashion? What are the most likely applications?

J. **FORM & FUNCTION** – What possible physical forms will the solution have? Specify in detail. How does form relate to function? How would a user be affected by form or function? What are the possible functional uses?

K. **SUPPORT** – Are there delivery, insurance, licensing, manufacturing, outsourcing, packing, storage, tracking, training, or transportation considerations?

L. **CONSTRAINTS** – What constraints are there? How would constraints influence function? If you varied some of the constraints, can you think of other uses? What if some constraints were removed would the idea or uses change?

These questions epitomize the scrutiny principles: does the proposed solution address the requirements of the problem? Where does the idea fall short of solving the problem? Are there any inconsistencies in the proposal? Do all the aspects of the idea make sense to you? Is the problem well defined? Are the objectives well understood? What are the main deliverables? Does the solution adequately address all the basic objectives of the problem? What scenarios, circumstances, and situations are likely to occur during operation? What experiments or tests should be performed that would adequately assess the feasibility of an idea? Are there any known shortcomings in the solution? These questions are designed to tease out the flaws in a solution so that these flaws can be addressed.

First, you considered the proposal looking for imperfections, pitfalls and flaws. Next, applications were considered. The objective of the scrutiny principle is to carefully consider an idea with the objective of improving the candidate proposal. The objective is not just to find flaws but make a solution acceptable and functional. By identifying shortcomings, you can address each of them with refinements. After applying the scrutiny principle, your solution or proposal should be more robust. Flaws that were identified can be addressed or designed around. Pitfalls can be avoided if they can be foreseen in advance.

EXPERIENCE – Experience encompasses your prowess, knowledge and history in a subject. Experience can be used to make good judgments because it can be used to identify issues with a proposal and suggest ways to address those issues. Experience can be used to help find new ideas or new avenues to explore when refining a proposal or process. Experience can serve as a teacher, it is a guide to the problem solver, and it is a life companion to the astute thinker.

Experience allows you to sidestep pitfalls because you will recognize similar problems previously encountered. Observe how others have resolved similar problems. Experience allows you to recognize the tell-tale signs of a problem long before a serious condition develops. Experience allows you to scrutinize solutions by identifying the parts of a solution that are likely to run into problems.

To make the best use of your experiences, keep a journal. Make notes to remind yourself of the lessons that you have learned. When you observe a similar situation again you will have a better idea of what to do the next time. You can also research what other people have done in similar predicaments. You can build upon those experiences and ultimately contribute to that body of learning.

How can you use experiences? The answer is a deliberate and conscious use of your experience to evaluate a situation or an idea. The use of experience, and knowledge to form an educated opinion serves as a guide to evaluating new ideas. Specific examples that worked in the past and those that failed will also help you assess proposals. Experience will help you make an educated guess as to whether a new idea will succeed or fail. Experience can suggest modifications to a proposal to improve your chances for success. However, experience only draws from historical examples. When paving new ground, it might be necessary to diverge from the past. In these cases, experience can be used to indicate avenues for exploration for possible scenarios that should be considered. Experience reminds us of pitfalls that pioneers fell into and how to avoid them. Experience illuminates the stumbling blocks and points the way towards a robust solution.

Ask yourself: Do any of my experiences indicate that something will fail in this solution? What examples can I draw from in my experience which may indicate that there may be an issue? From the experience of others that have encountered similar problems what did they do to solve the problem? From your experience, have other similar proposals been made in the past and why were they successful or unsuccessful? What pitfalls occurred in the past which might happen again? How does the present situation depart from the past that you have experience with? How would those differences play a role in the present solution? If a previous attempt failed, what lessons were learned by from the previous attempts?

FALLACIES OF THINKING – The fallacies of thinking are described in the next chapter. Fallacies of thinking are errors in logical thinking (Bennett, 2012). They can betray the logical validity of an argument. These thinking are related to Fire thinking because they are mental hazards that should be steered away from. As a cohesive body of knowledge, the fallacies of thinking are best described with their own chapter. It will be helpful to familiarize yourself with them.

OBJECTIVITY – Objectivity is the analysis of a problem free of preconceived notions. Bias is a partiality towards one thing over another. Impartiality are desirable when making judgments and applying scrutiny for an analysis. If you are biased before evaluation, you miss out on valuable ideas.

If you are trying to investigate a subject, or scrutinize a proposal, you want to evaluate without bias. If you are digging for the truth, you want to connect with reality. The analysis needs to be free of individual bias, or personal interpretation. Having bias for a specific solution without any logical basis will lead you astray.

The objectivity principle seeks to make conclusions that are free of bias. You want to be a neutral observer of the subject matter. Your analysis should arrive at an understanding of reality without interjecting your personal bias. You want to evaluate an idea free from of your personal prejudice.

To practice this, you should look at the subject or idea and try to identify where your bias may have crept in. In identifying where you have bias, you can take a step back and identify the broader context. You might also see that you are being influenced by external factors. Are these external influencers acceptable? How have these changed your perceptions?

To try to identify your biases, ask yourself the following questions: Am I partial to a specific solution even if the facts do not support that conclusion? Are there other ideas that have strongly influenced my decisions? Who stands to benefit the most? What are the core issues? What solution would best solve the problem? Have I been neutral in my analysis? Do I favor one idea without any cause or reason? What are the prejudices that have altered your thinking about an issue or solution? Do I have an emotional connection with a specific proposal?

WISDOM – Wisdom is the soundness of an action or decision using experience, knowledge, and good judgment. Wisdom is marked by learning from your past experiences and the ability to identify situations where you can apply your learning. Wisdom is also developed by learning from other people's mistakes and avoiding those mistakes yourself.

Wisdom is the body of knowledge and principles in a society which express sagacity, sophistication, and common sense. Living wisely entails integrating into society and contributing to its achievements. By working with others in a society, people benefit themselves through helping others. This is the most basic secret to success in life. Man is a social creature that flourishes when contributing to society.

Wisdom is typified by the following virtues: attentiveness, compassion, commitment, curiosity, dedication, empathy, equanimity, fairness, generosity, humility, integrity, kindness, nurturance, patience, peacefulness, respect, responsible, self-acceptance, and truthfulness. These qualities characterize wisdom because they result from a lifetime of applying experiences intelligently. Cultivating these qualities fosters the development of wisdom and sagacity.

Wise people are cultivated because in learning from history, we learn more about ourselves and the potential of human possibilities. Wise people are good listeners because comprehension is gained by learning. Listening is the social glue which connects people. Wise people use the institutions of society to do great things. They are willing to express a vision and improve the world. They are willing to lead, and work with others to make things happen. Wise people are open-minded, they are willing to question their assumptions, and try new things. Wise people focus on problem solving. They can focus on the core issues and see the big picture over the details. Wise people reflect.

Applied experience is wisdom. The use of our knowledge and experiences to predict outcomes and make smart decisions is a mark of good judgment. We are all a product of our choices in life. If at every major fork in the road, you make the best choice you can with the knowledge at hand you have lived a wise life.

When you settle on a decision, ask yourself what does your experience have to say about this matter? Can you use your experience as a guide for future action and decisions? What have other people done in similar situations? Will this harm others? Who stands to benefit from this decision? How will this decision affect the future? How can you make the best decision possible? How can I employ compassion and fairness in this situation? How committed and dedicated am I to this endeavor? If this is an ordeal, how can I be more patient? Am I being true to my ideals? Will I accept responsibility for the consequences of this decision? Does this problem really matter? How will this affect society at large?

Good judgment is act of arriving at sensible conclusions. Judgment transforms experience into wisdom by: thinking fallacies, experience, objectivity, scrutiny and wisdom. Scrutiny is the critical assessment and examination of an idea. The thinking fallacies allows you to sidestep mental traps. Experience is your prior knowledge on a subject that allows you to predict outcomes and avoid pitfalls. Objectivity allows you to analyze a situation without bias. Wisdom is the ability to apply experience, knowledge and good judgment to actions and decisions.

FIRE THINKING – JUDGMENT		
FIRE COMPONENT	**PRINCIPLE**	**DESCRIPTION**
JUDGMENT	Experience	Experience encompasses your prowess, skill, knowledge and history in a subject. These are used to make good judgments.
	Fallacies of Thinking	The fallacies of thinking are mental traps which are good to avoid in the evaluation process.
	Objectivity	Bias is a partiality, favoritism, and prejudice towards one thing, person, or idea over another. Objectivity and impartiality free of bias are desirable when making judgments.
	Scrutiny	Scrutiny is the critical assessment and examination of an idea or proposal. You can assess the quality of a solution through its relevancy, efficacy, usefulness and benefits with respect to a problem. The objective of scrutiny is to carefully assess a thing, idea, situation, or proposal.
	Wisdom	Wisdom is the soundness of an action or decision regarding the application of experience, knowledge, and good judgment. Wisdom is the body of knowledge and principles in a society which express sagacity, prudence, sophistication, and common sense.

Table 28 - Fire thinking Judgment component principles

Chapter 20 –Fallacies of thinking

The logical fallacies of thinking are mental traps and pitfalls that can occur during reasoning (Bennett, 2012). With practice, you will be able to identify them in logical arguments, analysis, and debates. These are easy mistakes to make, and people who are unaware of the logical fallacies of thinking often fall prey to them. They will play a critical role in your development of Fire thinking and judgment skills. Used wisely, the logical fallacies will serve as a life companion sniffing out phony assertions, mental manipulation, and faulty conclusions (Bennett, 2012).

To avoid the pitfalls presented by the fallacies of reasoning, it is important to understand that two kinds of errors threaten your thinking. The first are errors that affect the truth of your ideas. In this case, most of those errors can be eradicated through an application of the fallacies of reasoning. This type of thinking error applies to the truth of the premise or assertions. Errors that affect the truth of an argument can be found by testing the accuracy of individual statements.

The second type of error in thinking is related to reasoning. These kinds of error cripple the argument's validity. The legitimacy of the reasoning that delivered the conclusion is questionable. The process of reasoning you employ affects the conclusions you arrive at. Your thinking journey is as vital as the destination. The methods and tools are the means to different ends. Good thinking paves the way to good results.

Logical fallacies related to reasoning do not occur within the formulation of logical statements. Rather, they occur in the reasoning used to solve your problem. Like a disease, these errors infect and taint your thinking. There are wide variety of fallacies associated with faults in reasoning which include fallacies related to evidence, claims, logical assertions, generalizations, poor conclusions, premises, and red herrings. Therefore, to assess whether a line of reasoning is valid, you need to examine the steps that you took to solve your problem. You must ferret out these errors in reasoning.

You can root out many kinds of errors in thinking using the logical fallacies. Use of the logical fallacies of reasoning will guide you safely through the maze of thinking traps. Practice familiarizing yourself with the logical fallacies. Drilling, observation, practice, reconsolidation, reinforced experiences, repetition, and training are how the human mind learns. Strive to make the ability to see logical fallacies of thinking second nature to you.

The Greek philosopher Aristotle identified 13 fallacies in his work *On Sophistical Refutations* (Aristotle, On Sophistical Refutations (Sophistici Elenchi), 2015). He identified six linguistic fallacies: the fallacy of accent (#26), amphiboly (#18), equivocation (#24), composition (#20), division (#22), and figure of speech (#29). He highlighted seven non-linguistic fallacies. These were the fallacy of accident (#17), affirming the consequent (#1), in a certain respect (#12), ignorance of refutation (#31), begging the question (#43), false cause (#54), and many questions (#21). The numbers correspond to their descriptions that follow.

A full description of the Logical Fallacies of thinking are described in the Full Edition of the Four Elements of Thinking. Many apps, on-line websites and other books have also described the Fallacies. To save space in this Pocket Edition of the Four Elements of Thinking they are each only given a brief description.

1. **AFFIRMING THE CONSEQUENT** – If a consequence (effect) is true that doesn't mean the antecedent (cause) is true. If X is true, then Y occurs. I observe Y. The error is to conclude that X has happened. There might be other causes to Y.

2. **ARGUMENTUM AD BACULUM** – People accept the truth based on sound reasoning and logical arguments, not physical threats or coercion. The threat of physical violence does not make statement true.

3. **ARGUMENTUM AD CONSEQUENTIAM** – Disagreeable consequences do not disprove agreeable arguments. Also, agreeable consequences do not prove disagreeable arguments.

4. **ARGUMENTUM AD HOMINEM** – Attack the argument, not to the person making the argument. A rational thinker will separate the person from the issue.

5. **ARGUMENTUM AD IGNORANTIAM** – Do not assume something that might be true is true. Because no one can prove a thing false does not make it true. An argument is not invalid just based on disproving a nonessential part of it.

6. **ARGUMENTUM AD MISERICORDIAM** – An appeal to pity to gain sympathy and favor will not make a statement true nor can it replace logical reasoning.

7. **ARGUMENTUM AD POPULUM** – Collective belief by the general populous does not make something true. This fallacy is also known as appeal to the masses, appeal to the majority, the bandwagon fallacy, and others.

8. **ARGUMENTUM AD VERECUNDIAM** – Prestige does not equate with factual evidence. Assertions should align with evidence.

9. **COMPLEX CAUSE** – Many events or effects often have numerous, complex causes. Some problems take numerous scientists and researchers and decades of investigation to make headway.

10. **CONTRARY TO FACT CONDITIONAL ERROR** – Alter your conclusion to fit the facts; do not alter the facts to fit a conclusion.

11. **DENYING THE ANTECEDANT** – An effect will not happen if all the necessary causes are not present. This can be expressed as: If P, then Q. Not P, Thus Q.

12. **DICTO SIMPLICITER** –This error in thinking is committed when a general rule is applied to all situations even when there clearly are exceptions to the rule. Do not apply general rules to the exception.

13. **ARGUMENT FROM IGNORANCE** –This fallacy is committed when a conclusion is based primarily on lack of evidence to the contrary. Absence of evidence is not evidence of absence.

14. **EXISTENTIAL FALLACY** – A specific conclusion drawn from a universal premise is not necessarily true. Not all universals need to have a specific example. This can be expressed as: All X are Y. All Z are X. Thus, some Z are Y.

15. **EXPLICIT** - Be explicit when producing descriptions. It is easy to make a logical error in thinking if two parties do not have the same understanding of the definition of something.

16. **FAILURE TO ELUCIDATE** – This logical fallacy is also known as *obscurum per obscurius*. If a definition is more difficult to understand than the concept being defined, then the definition is not clear.

17. **FALLACY OF ACCIDENT** – Hasty generalizations turn isolated instances into universal principles without sufficient evidence.

18. **FALLACY OF AMPHIBOLY** – Amphiboly occurs when the construction of a sentence allows for two different meanings. It occurs when a conclusion is drawn from an unclear phrase with multiple definitions or multiple interpretations.

19. **FALLACY OF ANTHROPOMORPHISM** – Do not apply human endowments to an animal, or inanimate objects. Attributing human emotion to animals or inanimate things as a literary device is acceptable in a creative context.

20. **FALLACY OF COMPOSITION** – Properties and characteristics of the part are not necessarily shared by the whole. This can be expressed as: A is a part of B. A has property X. Thus, B has property X.

21. **FALLACY OF COMPOUND QUESTIONS** – A question with embedded assumptions is often more of a statement than a question. The loaded question is misleading because a hidden assumption is implicit in the question.

22. **FALLACY OF DIVISION** – Properties of the whole are not necessarily exhibited by the parts of that whole. Reverse of the fallacy of composition, expressed as: A is a part of B, B has property X. Thus, A has property X.

23. **FALLACY OF EMOTIVE LANGUAGE** – The stimulation of emotion will not make a true logical statement false, nor will it make a false statement true. Loaded language are used to elicit an emotional response in place reasoning.

24. **FALLACY OF EQUIVOCATION** – This fallacy is also known as doublespeak. A single word or phrase that has multiple meanings is used to cause ambiguity. The ambiguity can cause confusion and result in erroneous conclusions to be drawn.

25. **FALLACY OF EXCLUSION** – Do not exclude or alter relevant facts when considering a problem.

26. **FALLACY OF VICIOUS ABSTRACTION** – This logical fallacy is also known as contextomy, fallacy of accent and quote mining. Quoting something out of context often distorts its original meaning.

27. **FALSE ANALOGY** – Analogies are just examples. Taken too far, they produce false conclusions.

28. **FALSE DILEMMA** – When given a dilemma with two options, often a third option exists. When presented with a black and white situation, look for shades of grey.

29. **FIGURE OF SPEECH FALLACY** – Confusion can arise based on choice of wording. Choice of wording can manipulate the truth. The ordinary sense of the word is confused with the metaphorical, figurative or technical sense of the word.

30. **GENETIC ERROR** – Facts remain valid even if they originate from a non-credit worthy source. The argument should be evaluated on the strength of the evidence and its construction, not necessarily on the person making the argument.

31. **IGNORATIO ELENCHI** – To prove the wrong point is not the point. This fallacy is also known as a red herring, drawing an irrelevant conclusion, an irrelevant thesis, creating a smokescreen, and misdirection among others.

32. **INCONSISTENCY FALLACY** – Two contradictory statements cannot both be true. Two contradictory premises cannot both be true. This is also known as Kettle logic and internal contradiction.

33. **INDUCTION AND DEDUCTION** – Good thinkers learn how to use induction and deduction. Deduction starts from the general and proceeds to the particular. Induction starts with particulars and proceeds to the general.

34. **INSIGNIFICANT CAUSE** – Many events have multiple causes. Some insignificant causes have no causal significance.

35. **INSUFFICIENT EVIDENCE** – Gather sufficient evidence to base your conclusions on. Refer to chapter 11 on evidence as an Earth thinking component.

36. **FALLACY OF JOINT EFFECT** – Some effects may have two causes. If both of these effects are not identified and acknowledged, then an error in reasoning might occur. This is also called common cause or confounding factors.

37. **LIMITED DEPTH** – Individuals who belong to a group still have individuality. In this logical fallacy, membership in a category is used in lieu of a rational explanation.

38. **LIMITED SCOPE** – Theories that explain only one occurrence of something might be too limited in scope. If a theory only explains a single phenomenon, it is likely to be inadequate.

39. **NON-SEQUITUR** – Eliminate any point or piece of data that has no bearing on the current problem. The conclusion does not follow from the premises.

40. **NON-SUPPORT** – Manipulated evidence subverts the conclusion. An explanation is offered but the evidence is biased or ad hoc evidence.

41. **OCCAM'S RAZOR** – Try the simplest explanation first. Refer to chapter 14 on Abductive reasoning as an Earth thinking component. Occam's razor is a principle of that component.

42. **PETITIO PRINCIPII** – Do not begin with a conclusion. *Petitio principii* in Latin means "assuming the initial point". The logical form of this fallacy is: assume X to be true. Thus, we can conclude that X is true.

43. **POST HOC ERGO PROPTER HOC** – The Latin phrase means "after this therefore because of this". Event, A, happens to precede event, B. But, this does not mean that A is necessarily a cause of B. Correlation is not causation.

44. **PREJUDICIAL LANGUAGE** – This fallacy is about substance over style. Clever rhetoric is not a basis for the truth. Loaded and emotional terms are used to attach value or moral virtue to believing in a proposition.

45. **SLIPPERY SLOPE** – In this logical fallacy, a series of causes and effects (causal chain) is assumed to inevitably lead to an undesirable outcome. Thus, the first step should not be taken.

46. **SLOTHFUL INDUCTION** - Inductive arguments start from particulars and proceed to the general. However, sometimes a preponderance of evidence may point to an incorrect conclusion.

47. **STRAW MAN FALLACY** – The straw man fallacy is committed when a person ignores the logical position of someone and substitutes a distorted, exaggerated, or misrepresented version of that position.

48. **SUBVERTED SUPPORT** – This logical fallacy attempts to provide an explanation for a phenomenon that does not exist or an explanation for a phenomenon with no evidence that it exists.

49. **BROAD DEFINITIONS** – Definitions that are too broad are not useful definitions. Logical thinking can go awry when definitions are too broad because it brings in items into a discourse that do not belong there.

50. **NARROW DEFINITIONS** - Definitions that are too narrow are not useful definitions. This happens when a definition does not include items that should be included.

51. **TU QUOQUE** – Two wrongs do not make a right. *Tu quoque* in Latin means "you also". It discredits an assertion made by one who fails to act consistently with a claim. It claims falsehood because one does not act in accordance with his claims.

52. **NOT TESTABLE** – If predictions fail, the theory should be changed to accommodate new information. The refutability of a theory is the inherent possibility that it could be proven false.

53. **WRONG DIRECTION** – In this fallacy, the cause and effect are reversed, the cause is claimed to be the effect and vice versa. It is also known as the fallacy of questionable cause or false cause.

Chapter 21 –Fire Thinking and Contingency

One of the aspects of Fire thinking is to consider unforeseen circumstances that may arise with a proposed solution. These potential problems can be address with a contingency plan. Thus, a contingency plan is a way to refine a candidate solution to account for possible disasters. Contingency planning requires foresight, planning, and anticipation. A contingency plan is developed through the consideration of probable worst-case scenarios that may arise.

VULNERABILITY – A vulnerable point is a susceptibility or liability with respect to a threat or hazard. The first thing to consider when developing contingencies is vulnerabilities. A good understanding of vulnerabilities will set the stage for Fire thinking and contingency plan development.

Vulnerabilities will vary based on the context of your problem. You need to first think of what the system under consideration is. It might be a group of people, a person, a website, or a physical structure. The nature of the vulnerabilities and hazards that you will consider depend on how you frame your problem, and how you delineate the boundaries of your system.

A vulnerable point in the system is where to start thinking about contingency plans. These are points in the system where things can go wrong. Malicious attackers, unfortunate disasters, or natural hazards can wreak havoc. Machines and computer systems need power and have physical vulnerabilities.

HAZARD – A hazard is a danger or risk. Hazards represent uncertainties and threats that can create a dangerous situation. The consideration of a hazard goes hand-in-hand with spotting vulnerabilities. Identifying hazards and vulnerabilities allow you to develop a response and contingency plan.

A hazard might be an attacker, a natural disaster, an unexpected event, an exception, threat, or problem cause by an accident. An attacker might be a malicious person or a deliberate antagonist. A hazard might also be a person who causes a problem accidentally or through inexperience. A natural hazard might include fire, extreme weather, earthquakes, and other weather-related effects. An unexpected event might include a child using the system. An operational exception case might be the use of the product in a way not designed for or not how it was intentionally designed to be used. Problems caused by accidents might include accidental fires, physical breeches, and physical damage through misadventure.

A hazard might be foreseeable or unforeseeable by the designers. A hazard might be preventable or unpreventable. A hazard might be random or deliberate. A hazard might be man-made or natural. A hazard might be effective against a specific vulnerability or broadly dangerous. A hazard might be physical, virtual, or electronic. A hazard might take the form of something financial, social, physical, or biological. You can only plan and prepare for hazards that are foreseeable, and preventable. A system can be fortified against man-made and natural disasters.

Standards are rules that systems must adhere to. Standards are often created by professionals who have dedicated their careers to thinking about contingency plans and potential hazards. When you are thinking about hazards, you should consider that there may already be institutions, policies or practices that you might can draw inspiration from for your situation.

RESPONSE – A response is a predefined reaction to a hazard. Responses are alternatives and adaptations that are used to mitigate the effect of a crisis. Responses can improve and redefine proposed solutions to a problem. After you identify a set of hazards, you can group them into categories. Then you can devise specific responses to individual hazards or groups of similar hazards.

The objective of designing responses is to address hazards. Responses are part of a contingency plan. Predefined responses provide premeditated alternatives during a crisis. When a hazard occurs, knowing what to do, who to contact and where to be can mean the difference between life and death. If you are thinking about a solution to a problem, developing responses and contingency plans can make a proposal more robust in the face of hazards. Predefined responses can focus your efforts in developing a solution. Training, resources, and equipment will be used more strategically by thinking about what hazards are likely to occur. When you think about overcoming obstacles and hazards related to a solution, it will be more obvious what materials, tools, resources, finances, people, knowledge, conditions, skills, or experts that are required to implement a proposal.

Responses are designed to protect against a specific hazard or a group of similar hazards. Hazards can exploit vulnerabilities in the system. Responses do one of four things. First, they allow the system or people to become aware of a hazard. Secondly, a response can manage the hazard. Third, a response can be designed to allow the system to recover from a hazard or mitigate the damage caused by a hazard. And finally, a response can be designed to anticipate a hazard that has not yet occurred or provide an indicator that a hazard is imminent. Thus, the primary functions of a response are to detect, manage, recover from, and anticipate hazards.

A. **HAZARD DETECTION** – A system or person cannot take any action if they are unaware of a hazard. Thus, the responses need to be able to detect the presence of a hazard and issue an alert.

B. **HAZARD MANAGEMENT** – The function of hazard management is to address the hazard. If possible, the response might be to remove the hazard. The response may try to eliminate vulnerabilities of a system being exploited by a hazard. The response might redirect, suppress, or alter the hazard itself.

C. **HAZARD RECOVERY** – Responses can be designed to consider recovery from hazards. Recovery from a hazard may include assessing the damage that was done, evaluating what is still functioning, what resources are available, containing collateral effects, and coordinating relief efforts. The purpose of hazard recovery is to mitigate the damage caused by the hazard and to restore order.

D. **HAZARD PREDICTION** – Hazard prediction looks for signs of an impending hazard. Preventative action can be taken when the indicators suggest trouble.

A response might be automated. Intelligent software might be employed to create an ever-vigilant sentinel system. Expert systems can be used which encode the responses that an expert might take when faced with a similar hazard. Algorithmic responses are used by automated systems which evaluate system inputs to determine a set of responses based on the hazard.

Consider the following factors when you are planning responses:

A. **ALARM** – How will people know there is a hazard in the first place? Can there be an alarm or notification put in place to notify first responders?

B. **ALTERNATIVES** – The design of responses requires thinking about alternatives. What are the possible alternatives that can address a specific hazard?

C. **AUTOMATION** – Sometimes an automated response can be used to address a hazard. An automated response has the advantage that a person does not need to be present for the response to activate. The response can be vigilant day and night.

D. **COLLATERAL DAMAGE** – Is there the potential for collateral damage if a hazard occurs? Will innocent bystanders be put in harm's way? Does the response to a hazard itself create a new hazard?

E. **CONTAINMENT** – How will a hazard be contained? When the hazard occurs how will the hazard be contained so that it does not spread?

F. **COORDINATION** – If the response is going to come from a group of individuals, how will they be coordinated? When coordination is needed, consider how people will communicate, divide tasks, and orchestrate activities.

G. **CONSTRAINTS** – Are there constraints to consider when crafting a response? Constraints may be physical, psychological, financial, systemic, spatial, temporal, informational, or skill based in nature.

H. **COST** – The cost of resources, equipment, manpower or services required to implement a response influences the scope of the response. If you prioritize your hazards, you can devote more resources to most dangerous hazards.

I. **EXISTING RESPONSES** – Are there already responses to similar types of hazards that others have developed that you can use? Are there procedures, products, training, studies, and companies already devoted to these hazards?

J. **HAZARD TYPE** – Can the hazards be grouped into categories? If so, perhaps a class of response can be created for each type of hazard. You might categorize your hazards into natural disasters, man-made hazards, accidents, software threats, physical defects, and malicious attackers.

K. **PREDICTION** – Can the system predict a hazard? Does the hazard have tell-tale signs indicating that it is about to occur? Can evacuation procedures be used when a disaster is eminent? What sort of indicators can be used to predict a hazard?

L. **PRIORITY** – During a hazard, what important things must be done and what priority should be given to those things such that an orderly response can be given instead of a chaotic one? In what order should the steps of a response be taken?

M. **RESPONSE TIME** – When it comes to hazards, a quick response time saves lives or mitigates the damage done by the hazard. The faster the response, the less time the hazard is given to spread or inflict collateral damage. Speed of the response is governed by training, available equipment, effective response procedures, and well-maintained tools.

N. **RESOURCES** – When you develop a response to a hazard, you need to consider the available resources. Resources may encompass capital, connections, equipment, licenses, manpower, partnerships, software, and training. Resources are money, material, equipment, and staff which can be mustered to address a hazard.

O. **ROLES & RESPONSIBILITIES** – Are there point guards that can be given roles or responsibilities when a hazard occurs? Consider the tasks that may need to happen when a hazard occurs. What evacuation procedures must be executed? What groups need to be coordinated? Who will contact first responders?

P. **SCOPE** – What is the extent of damage that the hazard is expected to pose? The expected extent of the hazard will govern the scope of the response. How will the hazard spread? How much collateral damage is the response expected to handle?

Q. **TRIGGER** – What will trigger the response to a hazard? When a hazard is detected, what will cause a response to that hazard to be enacted? A detection mechanism is a trigger. Some systems can detect a degradation that might eventually lead to a full-blown problem.

CONTINGENCY PLAN – A contingency plan is a procedure or set of activities to circumvent a crisis or obstacle. It is a prearranged strategy to respond to certain situations which have created hazards or obstacles. These plans need to account for the available resources and capabilities of the system. Once in place, these set of procedures can be institutionalized with a set of predetermined responses to challenges, obstacles, and hazards. During times of crisis, people may not have the wherewithal to muster a coherent response. The contingency plan can swoop in to provide a premeditated response to a crisis (Childs & Dietrich, 2002).

Contingency plans address two types of situations: hazards and consequences.

A. **HAZARD** – A hazard is a danger or risk. Hazards represent uncertainties and complications that can create a crisis or dangerous situation. A crisis is a period of intense difficulty, trouble or danger. Contingency plans are a set of responses created to contain, detect, predict and recover from hazards.

B. **CONSEQUENCES** – Contingency plans can also be used to take an alternate path when one path becomes unavailable. Sometimes the event is an accident or an unforeseen problem. Other times, the event might be something that you had anticipated might happen. Either way, the consequence of that event has resulted in an obstacle that requires you to circumvent it with a contingency.

Contingency plans are a set of responses assembled to address a crisis or a consequence. The response principle of the contingency component of Fire thinking is used to create the responses to hazards. In addition, there are several key considerations when developing contingency plans.

A. **OPERATIONS CONTINUITY** – A contingency plan should account for continuity of operations. When a hazard or an unforeseen consequence strikes, you want to get back to business as usual as soon as possible.

B. **HAZARD RESPONSES** – A contingency plan is a collection of responses as described in the response principle of the contingency component. A response is a predefined reaction to a hazard. Responses are alternatives and adaptations that are used to mitigate the effect of a crisis. Responses are designed to detect, manage, recover from, and anticipate hazards. First, responses are used to detect a hazard and notify people of that hazard. Secondly, responses manage hazards. Third, responses are used to recover from a hazard and mitigate damage caused by a hazard. Finally, responses anticipate hazards that have not yet occurred or provide an indicator that a hazard is imminent.

C. **INFRASTRUCTURE PROTECTION** – A contingency plan should consider the infrastructure and how to protect it. Infrastructure is defined as the physical and organizational structures needed for the operation of an enterprise. If you are developing a contingency plan, consider what would happen the infrastructure were unavailable. How you would protect the most vital infrastructure.

D. **CRISIS COMMUNICATIONS** – During a crisis, communications might be limited. A contingency plan should take into consideration the possibility of limited communications between people and organizations.

E. **ALTERNATE PLANS** – At the very heart of contingency planning is the creation of alternate paths when one path becomes unavailable. When one option is no longer viable, are there other options that can be considered? What happens when a crisis arises which causes your original plans to go awry? When an unforeseen consequence occurs because of a disastrous event how can you get back on track? Planners often include alternate dates or plans in case catastrophe strikes.

Contingency plans are designed to address a crisis or unforeseen consequence (Childs & Dietrich, 2002). They are typically developed in advance when careful thought can be given to a hazard and its appropriate response before disaster strikes. Contingency plans pull together all the other principles of the contingency component of Fire thinking. Contingency plans provide another option when one option becomes unavailable.

The contingency component is comprised of: vulnerabilities, hazards, responses, and contingency planning. The first step is to understand the

<u>vulnerabilities</u> in a system. These will be points where a system is susceptible to hazards. <u>Hazards</u> can create dangerous situations arising in a crisis. A <u>response</u> is designed which aims to specify a predefined reaction to a hazard. Responses are designed to detect, manage, recover from, and anticipate hazards. Responses are used detect and then notify people of a hazard. Responses define ways to manage hazards when they occur. Responses are used to recover from or mitigate the damage caused by a hazard. Responses anticipate hazards that have not yet occurred. Finally, <u>contingency plans</u> are created to define a prearranged strategy to respond to a hazard. A contingency plan is a set of procedures that provide an alternate plan when options become unavailable due to a hazard. They are designed to respond to hazards and protect infrastructure in the face of limited resources and under duress. Contingency planning encourages you to think about alternatives, weaknesses, vulnerabilities, and spurs you to develop responses.

FIRE THINKING – CONTINGENCY		
FIRE COMPONENT	**PRINCIPLE**	**DESCRIPTION**
CONTINGENCY	Vulnerability	A vulnerable point is a susceptibility or liability with respect to a threat or hazard.
	Hazard	A hazard is a danger or risk. Hazards represent uncertainties and complications that can give rise to a crisis.
	Response	A response is a predefined reaction to a hazard. Responses are alternatives and adaptations that are used to mitigate the effect of a crisis. Responses are designed to detect, manage, recover from, and anticipate hazards. Responses can improve and redefine proposed solutions to a problem.
	Contingency Plan	A contingency plan is a procedure or set of activities. With respect to contingency planning, plans are a prearranged strategy to respond to a consequence or hazard. Plans need to consider the resources and capabilities of the system.

Table 29 - Fire thinking Contingency component principles

Chapter 22 –Fire Thinking and Validity

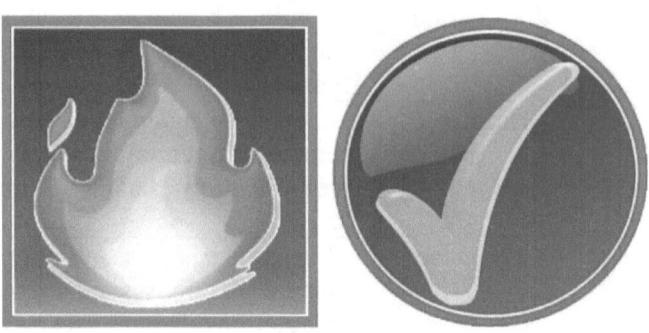

A branch of philosophy called Epistemology is devoted to the theory of knowledge. Epistemology is concerned with the methods, validity, and scope of knowledge. It endeavors to determine what knowledge is, and how it can be acquired, and the extent to which a subject can be known. It is also concerned with methodology, and the ways that one can use to try to understand something. Fire Thinking evaluates the validity and reliability of an idea or knowledge.

Trochim (Trochim, 2001) defined *validity* as, "the best available approximation to the truth of a given proposition, inference, or conclusion" (p 20). He defined four types of validity: *conclusion validity, internal validity, construct validity, and external validity.*

Conclusion validity is concerned with the relationship between a cause and an effect (Trochim, 2001). It tries to determine if multiple conclusions could be drawn from a hypothesis. If you are considering two things, is there some relationship between those things that allows you to draw a conclusion about them?

Internal validity deals with the extent that one thing causes another (Trochim, 2001). The causal relationship between two things determines its internal validity. Conclusion validity asserts that there might be a relationship, and internal validity tries to ascertain the causality in that relationship. Does some effect have multiple causes?

Construct validity deals with testing for internal validity and conclusion validity (Trochim, 2001). It is concerned with how well a test can determine a causal relationship between two things. Construct validity develops experiments to test for a causal relationship. Construct validity verifies conclusions.

External validity is concerned with the ability to generalize causal relationships to other persons, places, and times (Trochim, 2001).

STANDARDS (CRITERION OF TRUTH) – Criteria of truth are standards used to judge the truthfulness of a claim. Fire thinking uses this as a tool of verification. These tests of truth separate truth from falsehood. A *standard* is a measure by which evaluations can be compared against. It is a widely accepted baseline norm. Typical criteria of truth are: authority, coherence, consensus gentium, correspondence, mere consistency, naïve realism, pragmatism, and strict consistency (Sahakian & Sahakian, 1993).

A. **AUTHORITY** – Professionals or those with experience and training in a specific area of knowledge are often used as criteria of truth. Their experience, knowledge and familiarity command respect and allow their statements to serve as yardsticks by which to judge decisions and proposals. However, be careful not to fall prey to *argumentum ad verecundiam*. This is a fallacy of thinking.

B. **COHERENCE** – Coherence provides a consistent explanation for all the available facts. Scientists use coherence by integrating all the pertinent facts of a subject into a consistent and cohesive body of knowledge. It provides the most coherent explanation for all the available observations and facts.

C. **CONSENSUS GENTIUM** – General agreement by nearly all people that a certain viewpoint is true. It is the universal consent of all mankind. Because all humans hold a common belief, that notion can be used as a criterion on truth. It should be used cautiously as a criterion of truth because it is not infallible. Beware of *argumentum ad populum*, a fallacy of thinking.

D. **CORRESPONDENCE** – Correspondence is defined as a claim that matches with its object. Correspondence is generally accepted to be the most valid of the criteria of truth. Tests of truth determine the degree of similarity between what is posited and what actually exists in objective reality. The scientific method often uses experiments, hypothesis and tests to ascertain correspondence.

E. **MERE CONSISTENCY** – Mere consistency is a set of statements that are self-consistent. The assertions do not contradict each other. Mere consistency is a necessary condition for the truth of any argument. By itself, mere consistency is insufficient as a criterion because it only considers part of a problem. It can assist in reconciling evidence into a coherent whole.

F. **NAÏVE REALISM** – Naïve realism asserts that only phenomenon which is directly observable by the human senses is true. First-hand observation determines the truth of *any* statement. It is an insufficient criterion of truth because there are many phenomena which are true but not observable by the human senses. Human senses can be fooled such that perceptions do not match reality. Though, direct observation can often serve as valuable data points to take into consideration.

G. **PRAGMATISM** – Pragmatism uses real world efficacy as a yardstick for truth. If an idea works, then it must be true. The successfulness of an applied solution is demonstration of its truth. Pragmatism may also generate false positives. Some solutions may appear to work, but other factors were the actual reason for success.

H. **STRICT CONSISTENCY** – Strict consistency are a set of claims such that one statement logically follows another. Formal logic and syllogisms are examples of strict consistency. It can examine a set of propositions. However, it may produce stray results which lack coherence and are incomplete.

There are also false or inadequate criterions of truth (Sahakian & Sahakian, 1993). These are often used by people unconsciously as a criterion of truth. However, from a logical stand-point they are inadequate as true measures of determining truth. Be wary when someone wields one of these false criterions of truth. The erroneous criterions of truth are: custom, emotions, instinct, intuition, majority rule, revelation, time, and tradition.

A. **CUSTOM** – Custom is often used as an informal criterion of truth. However, analytically, customs are not considered a valid test of truth. People assume that if they do what is customary and popular it must be valid basis for wisdom and truth.

B. **EMOTIONS** – Emotions are often used as a basis for swaying judgment even in the face of contrary evidence. Feelings are not an adequate test for truth. Emotions are fickle and can cloud judgment when evaluating knowledge. Emotions do play a role in decisions because humans are emotional. Emotions develop because of an emotional investment, or personal relationship. When making judgments, express your emotions and search your feelings. There may be a rational reason driving your emotions that is an actual criterion of truth.

C. **INSTINCT** – Instincts are not accepted as reliable criterion of truth because of their emotional content, fickleness, and vagueness. Instincts have not been used in logical analysis, debate, or as a criterion of truth. The basic drives, such as thirst may influence your decisions but should not serve as a basis for ascertaining truths.

D. **INTUITION** – Intuition is a judgment that is not dependent on a rational examination of the facts. Intuition is often a flash of insight, an epiphany that delivers a solution. Intuitive sensations often provide answers which turn out to be true. Intuition can be a wellspring for truths, rather than a criterion with which to judge truths.

E. **MAJORITY RULE** – Majority rule is a statistical method of accepting assertions and proposals. Truth by consensus is usually a poor determinant of truth. It often gives rise to *argumentum ad populum,* a fallacy of thinking.

F. **REVELATION** – Revelation is a truth which originates from a "higher power" such as a deity. Many religions depend on revelation as a test of truth. Revelation may serve an individual but is inadequate as a coherent proof of knowledge.

G. **TIME** – Time is often erroneously used as a criterion of truth. Something which stands the test of time may be useful as practical knowledge but may be false. Passage of time will not necessarily overturn erroneous beliefs. Hence, time is an insufficient test for truth in the same way that tradition and customs are.

H. **TRADITION** – Tradition is a standard which is held by a group of people through generations. Tradition is a powerful social mechanism. However, it is possible for falsehood to be passed down generationally. Tradition emphasizes historical context over critical evaluation.

CONSISTENCY (CONSTRUCT VALIDITY) – Construct validity gauges if a measure is consistent with the theoretical concept being measured (Trochim, 2001). Tests of validity are designed to support or refute the construct validity. When you are considering the validity of a study and its attendant measurements, consistency between expected outcomes and actual outcomes gives an indication of its validity.

Trochim defines construct validity as alignment between the intended study and the actual study implemented (Trochim, 2001). It also implies congruity in the expected measurements of the outcomes and the ones that were measured. Construct validity is considered after it has been established that there is a relationship between two variables which is called conclusion validity. Afterwards, internal validity implies there is a causal relationship between two variables. Finally, construct validity is used to generalize these relationships.

Construct validity is consistency in what you measure and the results that you observe. How can you demonstrate the validity of a hypothesis or theory? One of the key principles is through construct validity. Consistency of outcomes increases the confidence that the assertions are true. Consistency gives rise to validity. Validity is one of the fundamental components of Fire thinking because it allows you to judge an idea effectively. Is the hypothesis, proposal, idea, or theory believable and reasonable? Do the experiments trying to validate the hypothesis produce consistent results? Do feasibility studies validate the proposed solution?

Fire thinking is about using good judgment. Good judgment involves making intelligent decisions, and consideration of the evidence that you have available to gauge its validity before coming to conclusions. Snap judgments, first impressions, and quick thinking have their place and sometimes it is necessary to do that particularly in times of crisis, competition, or emergency. However, measured, careful, and thoughtful judgments are often needed to make meaningful progress on projects, in the development of ideas and in professional practice. The validity component of Fire thinking adds the question, "is that really true?" to your repertoire of thinking tools. Don't take opinion and conjecture at face value. Dig up the evidence. Look for proof which can confirm or deny a viewpoint. What evidence is there which corroborates the assertions being made? Why should someone accept the notions being put forth? How can the claims be verified, substantiated or affirmed? Those questions get to heart of the validity component of Fire thinking.

PREDICTION – Prediction is being able to foretell a future event or trend. The forecast is inferred from evidence, knowledge, and experience. Valid information has a cause-and-effect relationship that has predictive value.

The predictive value of an equation, a theory, a hypothesis, an experiment has value to the scientist which uses these to build up a body of knowledge about the world. The predictive value of applied sciences, mechanics (statics, dynamics, and kinematics), thermodynamics, and the behavior of electronic and software components is useful to the engineer. The predictive value of a marketing study, social trends, competitive intelligence, and branding dynamics have value to the product manager. This predictive capability suggests that a group of individuals will generally behave in a certain way. It can forecast the likely trends that will become popular. How people might behave as a group.

An equation is the quintessential expression of predictability. An input goes into the equation and a predictable outcome is calculated. Entire careers are devoted to mathematically model the behavior of various systems or natural phenomena. A model tries to abstract the essential aspects of a system and capture that in a software program or set of equations so that engineers and scientists can study the system or phenomena under controlled conditions. Prediction finds uses in actuarial sciences, demographics, observational astronomy, machine learning, nuclear physics, predictive analytics, predictive systems modeling, regression analysis (statistics), and queuing theory.

Consider for your problem or subject matter, what are the central ideas and information that you depend upon to be predictable and valid? What ideas have you generated from Air thinking, and data have you dug up from Earth thinking that you hold to be valid? Why are these conjectures true? Can I predict the behavior of this event, mechanism, or phenomena? If I perform this experiment again will the outcome be the same? Can I draw upon the knowledge of mankind to help me develop a way to predict the outcome? From the mundane predictability of tossing a ball up and down to the extraordinary feat of throwing a space probe to another planet, predictability is part and parcel of validity and Fire thinking.

RELIABILITY – Reliability is consistency of results. *Reliability* was defined by Trochim (Trochim, 2001) as the consistency and dependability of a measure. It is how often you would get the same results from a measure given that the associated underlying phenomena were constant.

Validity is concerned with the truth of information. Reliability is concerned with the quality of information. Reliability as a consistency of a measure plays a vital role in statistics, science and mathematics. A measure is reliable if it produces similar results under consistent conditions. This is important if you are trying to analyze measured data and calculate statistics on them.

Consider for your investigation, where does reliability come into play? In what aspects of your problem is dependable knowledge important? Why would consistency of results matter? What can you do to ensure that procedures, practices and measurements are consistent? Consider the areas of your life where you depend on information such as schedules, measurements, and procedures to be reliable. In modern society, deliverables, inventory, and information need to arrive like clockwork at just the right time to fall into place with the rest of the system. Reliable deliverables, reliable knowledge, reliable measurements are part and parcel to modern society as well as the process of Fire thinking.

Share best practices to capitalize on the experience of others. Identify flaws in the way that measurements are taken to improve quality. Find methods that are effective and find ways to adapt them to your situation. Companies use software tools, create policies and define procedures for people to follow to improve production and testing quality. Successful companies identify methods that produce reliable results and they codify that into their culture.

For a more rigorous approach to validity calculation, researchers use statistical methods to ascertain a confidence level in a hypothesis. Trochim described establishing two mutually exclusive hypotheses which together encompasses all possible outcomes (Trochim, 2001). A *confidence level*, or alpha level, denoted by the Greek letter α is mathematically computed which gives a sense of whether you should reject or accept a theory. The *power*, denoted by the Greek letter β, is defined as the odds that a researcher will observe an effect when it occurs. From this, two types of errors can occur. A Type I error is a false positive which is the odds of claiming there was an effect when there was none. A Type II error is a false negative which is the odds of claiming there was no effect when there was one. There are many statistical methods such as the t-test, analysis of variance (ANOVA), analysis of covariance (ANCOVA), regression analysis, factor analysis, multidimensional scaling, cluster analysis, and discriminant function analysis that exist to determine a confidence level for a theory (Aczel & Sounderpandian, 2005). Scientific research progresses by means of predictable, reliable, and valid conclusions drawn from carefully designed repeatable experiments.

Fire thinking validity uses criterion of truth, consistency, prediction and reliability. Validity improves your ability to judge an idea. The first principle of validity is standards, or criterion of truth, which are the measures by which evaluations can be compared against. These are the widely-accepted baseline norms. The typical criteria of truth are authority, coherence, *consensus gentium*, correspondence, mere consistency, naïve realism, pragmatism, and strict consistency. The second principle is consistency, or construct validity, which is the consistency between measurements and observed results. Consistency of outcomes increases the confidence that the assertions are true. Third, the predictive value of evidence, knowledge, and experience should be considered in your analysis. Valid information is characterized by cause and effect relationships that have predictive value. Lastly, the reliability of a measure or information is how dependable and trustworthy it is. Repeated measurements are reliable if they consistently yield similar results.

FIRE THINKING – VALIDITY		
FIRE COMPONENT	**PRINCIPLE**	**DESCRIPTION**
VALIDITY	Standards (Criterion of Truth)	In epistemology, the criteria of truth are standards that are used to judge the accuracy of statements and claims. They are tools of verification. These tests of truth are used to separate truth from falsehood. A standard is a measure by which evaluations can be compared against. It is widely accepted baseline norm.
	Consistency (Construct Validity)	Construct validity gauges if the measure is consistent with the theoretical concept being measured. Tests of validity are designed to support or refute the construct validity.
	Prediction	Prediction is being able to foretell a future event or trend. The forecast is inferred from evidence, knowledge, and experience. Valid information has cause and effect information that has predictive value.
	Reliability	Validity and reliability go hand in hand. Reliability is the dependability and trustworthiness of a measurement. It is the degree to which the measure is consistent. Repeated measurements are reliable if they yield similar results.

Table 30 - Fire thinking Validity component principles

Chapter 23 – Problem Solving with the Four Elements

Now that you understand each of the four elements of thinking and their components, they can work together to solve problems, study a subject, make decisions, plan, and other cognitive tasks. This chapter describes a procedure for problem solving using the four elements of thinking.

It should be emphasized that most of the components of the four elements of thinking can be applied at all the stages of the problem-solving journey. Each section describing the elements of thinking components and principles were written with that in mind. However, the rest of this chapter suggests a specific path you can follow to tackle problems methodically until you become more familiar with each of the elements of thinking. Thought, reasoning and synthesis will remain versatile tools used throughout problem-solving. The basic steps of problem solving are:

STEP	DESCRIPTION
Problem Formulation	This step defines the problem or issue to be solved.
Knowledge	This is a base of accumulated knowledge that is relevant to the problem.
Solution Ideation	This step proposes solutions resulting from the various techniques for idea generation.
Selection	The candidate solutions are evaluated and selected through decision-making.
(Causes & Reasoning)	The root causes of the problem and logical reasoning can be applied throughout the problem-solving journey.
(Synthesis)	The components of synthesis thinking are used throughout problem-solving process.
Evaluation	In this step, proposed solutions are evaluated. Selected options can be documented and implemented and further evaluated.

Table 31 - Problem Solving steps using the Four Elements of Thinking

FOUR ELEMENTS PROBLEM SOLVING

1 PROBLEM FORMULATION

2 KNOWLEDGE

 EVIDENCE

 INVESTIGATE

 VALIDATION

5 CAUSES & REASONING

 DEDUCTION

 INDUCTION

 ABDUCTIVE REASONING

3 IDEATION

 INCUBATION

 INSIGHT

 INNOVATION

 CONTINGENCY

6 SYNTHESIS

 LINKING

 PERSPECTIVE

 PIVOTS

 SYNTHESIS

4 SELECTION

 DECISIONS

7 EVALUATION

 JUDGMENT

STEP 1 – PROBLEM FORMULATION

Problem formulation is perhaps the most important part of problem solving. It is the act of defining the problem to be solved. It defines a goal for the thinking journey. A problem is an unacceptable situation or a situation you want to improve. Problems are best phrased with a "How?" question. An issue is a matter that informed people disagree upon. An issue is best expressed using "Is", "Does", or "Should" as the leading word.

Consider some basic questions in defining the problem. What problem are you trying to solve? What issue needs to be addressed? Why is this a problem? Where is the problem encountered? Who are the relevant parties? When does the problem need to be resolved?

When developing a problem statement, try to be as specific as possible. A focused problem formulation will rally every other step in the problem-solving process. The problem statement defines what evidence is relevant. It determines which criteria are relevant in the selection step of problem solving.

After you have defined your problem, you can use the Problem redefinition principles of the Incubation component (Air thinking) to see if anything should be tweaked. Problem reformulation can be used to redefine a problem statement.

STEP 2 – KNOWLEDGE

Next, a good knowledge base will serve as a foundation to work from. Start with the Evidence component (Earth thinking) to build up a body of knowledge and facts that will be useful. Use the Investigate component (Air thinking) to creatively explore, experiment and inquire. Use the Validation component (Fire thinking) to verify that your evidence is valid and reliable. The problem statement defines the questions, and knowledge that is relevant.

STEP 3 – IDEATION

Solution ideation is the development of reasonable, practical, and effective solutions. In this step, ideas are generated which may potentially address the problem at hand. First, thoroughly study your body of evidence and investigation that resulted from Earth and Air thinking. Then, you can use the Incubation component (Air thinking) to let the information gestate. The techniques and principles of the Insight and Innovation components (Air thinking) can be used to stimulate creativity and create proposals. The Contingency component (Fire thinking) can be used to help analyze the problem and refine a proposal. The output of the ideation step should be one or more proposed solutions which could potentially solve the problem defined in the problem formulation step.

STEP 4 – SELECTION

Next, one of the proposed solutions is selected. The techniques of the Decisions component (Fire thinking) can be employed to help you select from among the proposed candidate solutions. The principles of the Decisions component are: goals, constraints, alternatives, criteria, consequences, and selection. The principles of the Decisions component are a step-by-step process of how to decide between various alternatives. The Judgment component (Fire thinking) can also be used to help evaluate candidate proposals.

A goal in decision-making is the ideal outcome for a decision; the solution which best solves the problem. Constraints identify limitations or restrictions. Alternatives, in this case, are the candidate proposals. Criteria are the factors that decisions are based upon. Consequences are the repercussions that would result from implementing a solution. Selection provides methods to choose between alternatives. For more details, refer to the Decisions component (Fire thinking) in chapter 18.

STEP 5 – CAUSES & REASONING

Throughout the entire problem-solving journey, the causes and logical reasoning can be used to make progress. The root causes of the problem are important to understand. They can indicate why the problem is happening and why there is an issue.

The Induction component (Earth thinking), Deduction component (Earth thinking) and Abductive reasoning component (Earth thinking) can be applied throughout the steps of problem-solving. They can steer what evidence is collected. The Assumptions principle (Induction), Causality and Decomposition principles (Abductive reasoning) can be used during the knowledge step of problem-solving. Reasoning can play a role in ideation. It can help in the Problem reformulation principle, Contemplation principle, Mental fluency principle and Innovation factors principles. Good reasoning can influence the selection of a proposal. The Selection principle (Fire thinking) is grounded in sound reasoning. Finally, reasoning can be applied to the evaluation of the effectiveness of a proposal.

STEP 6 – <u>SYNTHESIS</u>

Synthesis thinking can assist throughout problem-solving. All the components of Water thinking can be marshalled to provide deeper insight, a broader perspective, a greater understanding and wisdom to the problem at hand. The Linking component (Water thinking) can be used to associate concepts, cross-fertilize ideas, decompose the problem, and identify important patterns. These in turn could play a role during knowledge investigations, ideation, and selection. The perspective component (Water thinking) focuses on developing a big picture view, understanding the ecology of the problem, and a framework for working through the problem. Pivots (Water thinking) identifies the anchors, bottlenecks, catalysts tipping points and trends. These represent a vital understanding of the context and key ideas relevant to the problem. The Synthesis component (Water thinking) looks to compare, permute, and combine which can assist in solution ideation. It also tries to identify trade-offs and find compromises which can play a part in the selection process.

STEP 7 – <u>EVALUATION</u>

Finally, the evaluation step is used to refine the selected proposal. The proposal can be scrutinized for flaws with the aim of refining the solution. The Judgment component (Fire thinking) can be used to evaluate the selected proposal. The experience, fallacies, objectivity, scrutiny and wisdom principles of the Judgment component can refine a solution to be more robust, and practical. <u>Experience</u> can highlight pitfalls that might be encountered during implementation or guide the way towards an effective solution. The <u>fallacies</u> can spot if any logical flaws in thinking were made that need to be addressed. <u>Scrutiny</u> performs a critical assessment and examination of a proposal. <u>Wisdom</u> uses experience, knowledge and good judgement to cultivate a high-quality, wise, virtuous, and ethical solution.

Additionally, after a solution has been implemented, the effectiveness of the solution can be assessed. Future solutions can learn from the experience and wisdom gained from the difficulties of implementation.

The principles and components of the four elements of thinking are a set of mental tools. Together, these tools have the potential to solve any problem large or small. A master problem solver knows which mental tool is best suited to the cognitive task at hand. With practice, you will know which principle or component to use during the seven steps of problem solving.

Chapter 24 – Conclusion

The central idea of this book is to associate the classical four elements of earth, air, fire and water with the four principle aspects of thinking. Air representing lofty creativity. Earth representing grounded reasoning. Fire representing a blazing evaluation. Water representing a flowing synthesis. These four elements each give you a simple mnemonic, a memory tool, to help you to remember to apply these key aspects of thinking. The components and principles within each of the elements of thinking allows you to break down a complex problem, study a subject, and methodically arrive at a good solution or decision. Frequent use of the techniques of the four elements of thinking will improve your reasoning, creativity, and thinking aptitude.

Thinking is a skill that can be learned and practiced. Skills are developed through deliberate application. Practice leads to mastery. The principles within the elements provide techniques to focus your thinking in a methodical and structured fashion. Each of the elements of thinking imparts principles and techniques to improve your thinking skills. They break down a problem into manageable parts allowing you to focus on one aspect of thinking at a time. Frequently used skills become second nature. They become habit. Thinking elements remind you to employ all the dimensions of your mental faculties.

How often do you think about thinking? Thinking about thinking is not easy because it is hard to picture in your mind the concepts of creativity, reasoning, evaluation, and synthesis. These vital aspects of thinking are abstract and intangible which make them difficult to visualize. The thinking elements associate earth, air, fire and water to reasoning, creativity, evaluation and synthesis. The elements are easy to imagine because we routinely experience, see, feel, touch, hear, breathe and taste these things. The elements get you thinking about thinking because they are easy to picture in your mind's eye.

When you walk on earth, stride towards reasoning. Use a mental image of the planet Earth to prod you to engage your reasoning skills. When you see a park, a field, or a road think of gathering evidence, inductive reasoning, deduction, and abductive reasoning. You will gain confidence by using Earth thinking because your results will be grounded on solid reasoning. When you see stone and concrete, think of how you can apply reasoning to build a solid foundation for your analysis. Earth thinking builds up your case brick by brick to create an edifice of logic.

When you breathe air, exhale creativity. Feel the wind and envision clouds to remind you to employ creativity. Idea generation is at the heart of air thinking. You will be more resourceful using Air thinking. Picture the wind stirring to have it rustle your creativity. Picture a gust of air to launch your thinking with brainstorming and innovation. A gentle breeze to incubate ideas. A gale wind to push forth an investigation and exploration. A zephyr for mental flexibility and insight.

When you see fire, let the flames spark thoughts about evaluation. Envision a flame in your mind's eye to engage evaluation. Hold a mental image of a flame to refine understanding with evaluation. You will develop wisdom through Fire thinking. Picture an inferno to engage your judgement. Use the radiance of the sun to reach the truth through the validity component. Let the illumination of a fire be a north star for your decision making. See the blaze of a fire to use judgement. Let your mental fire burn away the debris from your thinking to allow for fresh growth.

When you drink water, gulp in synthesis. Capture in your mind's eye flowing water to apply synthesis thinking. Association with synthesis thinking. You will gain perspective by using Water thinking. See in your mind's eye, a river, an ocean, flowing water. As you see that mental image of water think about using synthesis thinking. See in your mind's eye a flowing river to remind you of the linking component circulating ideas. An ocean gives you a broad perspective. Imagine the source of a river to think of pivots. Picture a serene lake and think of synthesis giving life to your ideas.

Often, people do not know where to begin thinking about a problem. They go astray and get lost in the weeds of thought. They act on the first idea that comes to their mind without having all the facts, and without any methodical analysis. Earth thinking gives a thinker a starting place by collecting evidence, forming hypotheses, and setting off with a logical approach. Then, Air thinking jump-starts your creativity with original ideas and new avenues of investigation. Next, synthesis thinking finds the big picture perspective and identifies the pivotal aspects of a subject. It provides a map to guide the thinker in their journey. Lastly, Fire thinking illuminates the decisions and evaluates ideas. Evaluation is used to refine a solution, assess the truthfulness of claims, and create contingencies against potential mishaps.

A mechanic is only as good as the tools at his disposal to ply his trade. A composer combines the instruments of the orchestra to produce a symphonic masterpiece. The surgeon has a variety of implements to perform an operation on a patient. The artist has brushes and colors to create his magnum opus. The writer has words and plots as artistic implements. Likewise, the thinker is only as good his mental tools to help him work through a problem. The most vital tools in the thinker's toolbox are those of reasoning, creativity, synthesis and evaluation. The thinker uses these tools to solve, learn, innovate, synthesize and evaluate.

The elements of thinking encourage you to develop thinking skills using both sides of your brain. Some elements of thinking use the left brain (Earth, Fire), and some elements of thinking cater to the right side of the brain (Water, Air). Each side has strengths that complement the weaknesses of the other side. By learning the principles and techniques of the four elements of thinking, you will learn to utilize both sides of your brain better.

The *Earth* element of thinking represents reasoning. Earth thinking principles are used to logically and objectively reason through problems. Deduction, induction, and abductive thinking build upon a base of evidence. *Evidence* is the orchestration of facts, observations, investigation, details, concepts, and assumptions. *Induction* reasons from specific facts and observations to general principles (Copi, Cohen, & Flage, 2007). *Deduction* reasons from general principles to specific facts (Terrell, 1967). *Abduction* draws conclusions from the available evidence (Peirce, 1992). These reasoning components work with hypothesis, experimentation, evidence, logic, assumptions, argument, premise and syllogisms to arrive at conclusions. Deduction, induction and abductive reasoning are at the core of thinking about any subject. Sound reasoning provides a solid footing for any investigation. As with all the elements of thinking, remembering to use their principles separates a novice thinker from an experienced one.

The *Air* Element of thinking represents creativity and innovation. The creative aspects of thinking are used to generate original ideas, imaginative works, and alternatives. Air thinking uses a combination of curiosity, idea generation, intuition, exploration, and visualization. Together, these produce creative works, open new avenues of inquiry, find unorthodox approaches, and produce solutions. The Air thinking components are *investigation, incubation, insight* and *innovation*. Investigation spearheads the creative process by using curiosity, exploration, examination, inquiry and experimentation. *Incubation* is passive contemplation allowing the mind to gestate on a problem (Wallas, 1926). Incubation breaks conditioning, uses unconventional thinking, and reformulates problems to create eureka moments. *Insight* uses flexibility, intuition, mental fluency, perspective, and comparison to foster creativity. The *innovation* component uses brainstorming, collaborative creativity, and visualization to generate ideas. Air thinking techniques stimulates creativity and idea generation. Creativity is a fundamental mental faculty (Amabile, 1996). Everyone has the capability to be creative. Air thinking components and principles will develop and nurture your creative side.

The *Water* Element of thinking represents Synthesis. Synthesizing ideas involves the cross fertilization and bridging of concepts. Linking ideas allows you to organize and classify things (Barabasi, 2014). Water thinking classifies and sorts perceptions and information into concepts and knowledge. Synthesis is how we make sense of the world. Water thinking integrates concepts by connecting them into useful patterns. You are continually assimilating new ideas into existing patterns (Gharajedgaghi, 2005). This is a subtle, but fundamental aspect of the mind. Association, relations, and connections are how we navigate life and master social interactions. Water thinking seeks to methodically bring together different parts of your problem together. The key is to do so in an objective and unbiased manner. The goal of Water thinking is to take a step back, see the big picture, and connect different parts of your problem together. Water thinking is concerned with bridging concepts together, fitting pieces of the puzzle that go together, and identifying the big picture. Water thinking uses the linking, perspective, synthesis and pivots components. *Linking* uses association, cross fertilization, decomposition, organization and patterns principles. *Perspective* uses the big picture, system, framework, planning, and viewpoint principles. *Synthesis* is comprised of the compare & contrast, conclusion & summary, permutation & combination, thesis & antithesis, and tradeoffs & compromise principles. The pivots component uses the anchor, bottlenecks, catalyst, tipping point and trend principles. This ability to see the big picture is one of mankind's unique endowments.

The *Fire* Element of thinking represents evaluation. Fire thinking is used to make decisions, employ good judgement, create contingencies, and ascertain validity. Good *decision-making* defines goals, identifies constraints, assess alternatives, weighs criteria, considers consequences before selecting. Fire thinking promotes methodical and objective decision making by the best fit (Lehrer, 2010), devil's advocate, matrix method (Pugh, 1981), and feasibility focus selection techniques. The *judgment* component employs experience, objectivity, scrutiny, wisdom and awareness of thinking fallacies. Experience allows you to predict outcomes and avoid pitfalls. Objectivity fosters bias-free analysis. Scrutiny is the critical assessment of an idea. Wisdom is applied experience, knowledge and good judgment to actions. *Contingency planning* spots vulnerabilities and identifies hazards to develop appropriate responses (Childs & Dietrich, 2002). Contingency planning allows you to foresee and anticipate problems and enact a predetermined, methodical response to those hazards when they occur rather than try to develop a response under duress. Fire thinking is used to help you ascertain the *validity* of new information, ideas, and proposals. Standards, consistency, predictive value and reliability are the hallmarks of the validity component. When presented with new information, objective skepticism can be applied to evaluate the information. Air thinking is used to generate many alternatives, Fire thinking is used to select a good alternative when presented with a palette of choices.

Actions begin with thought. Masterpieces emerge from ideas. Wisdom arises from contemplation. Success develops from concentration. Science evolves from reasoning. Great pursuits spring from deep thought. Technology, societies, science, and math have all arisen from thinking. Landing on the moon (D'Antonio, 2008), taming atomic energy (Fermi, 1961), and the discovery of DNA (Watson & Crick, 1953) all started with but a thought. The mysteries of the universe both galactic and subatomic have been unraveled by human thought. At the heart of structured thought is reasoning, creativity, synthesis, and evaluation – the four elements of thinking.

Trouble occurs when action is undertaken without thought. The four elements of thinking are a mnemonic device to structure thinking. Earth thinking applies reasoning before reaching conclusions. Trouble occurs when conclusions are reached without reason. Air thinking applies creativity to generate ideas. Trouble occurs from ideas without exploration. Water thinking represents synthesis. Trouble occurs from analysis without perspective. Fire thinking focuses on evaluation and decision making. Trouble happens from decisions without consideration. Applying reasoning, creativity, synthesis, and evaluation urges you to think before you act. Knowledge comes from Earth thinking by reaching conclusions through reasoning. Success comes from Air thinking creating opportunity and value through creativity. Wisdom comes from Water thinking by meaningfulness through synthesis. Comprehension comes from Fire thinking seeking truth through evaluation.

Mastering your thoughts is the secret to success. It is the cornerstone of all endeavors. The four elements are a pathway to methodical thinking. Each of the essential four elements of thinking: reasoning, creativity, synthesis and evaluation will guide you through difficult problems, studying, mastering knowledge, and tackling everyday challenges. Earth thinking represents reasoning through logical analysis. Air thinking represents creativity and curiosity to generate ideas. Water thinking represents synthesis for linking, perspective, and pivots. Fire thinking represents evaluation for decision making, judgment calls, contingency planning, and assessing the truth. Life is a journey that requires thinking, learning, planning, and action. Success demands clarity of purpose, mental acuity, and methodical thinking as nurtured through the four elements of thinking. Voyages of discovery and personal mastery requires that you internalize the thinking elements making them second nature to you. Fortune favors the prepared mind. Methodical thinking is a skill developed through continued practice of the four elements. The four elements are mnemonic devices precisely to remind you to use them frequently. They provide the mental tools and techniques which pave the way to success. Let the four elements principles and components be your companion in the journey of life. They will guide you through life's challenges.

Part III – Component & Principles Summary

Appendix-1 – Earth Components & Principles Summary

EARTH THINKING – EVIDENCE		
EARTH COMPONENT	**PRINCIPLE**	**DESCRIPTION**
EVIDENCE	Assumptions	Something that is accepted to be true or certain to happen without proof.
	Gathering Evidence	Search in the internet, articles, journals, research papers, and books. Learn about the people, history, events, and available data.
	Organizing Information	Organizing facts relevant to your situation or problem. Store, sort, and index information for easy access.
	Assessment	Consider the accuracy and precision, interpretation and inference, relevance, reliability, subjectivity, objectivity, universals, and particulars of your gathered information.

Table 38 - Earth Thinking Evidence component principles

EARTH THINKING – DEDUCTIVE REASONING		
EARTH COMPONENT	**PRINCIPLE**	**DESCRIPTION**
DEDUCTIVE REASONING	Formal Logic	Formal logic is based on arguments involving deductive reasoning using relationships and including the use of syllogisms and mathematical symbols.
	Assumption	An assumption is something taken to be true or certain to happen without proof.
	Argument	An argument is a reason or set of reasons given with the aim of persuading others that an action or idea is right or wrong.
	Syllogism	A syllogism is a form of reasoning whereby a conclusion is drawn from two given or assumed propositions (premises). The conclusion may be valid or invalid. Each of the premises shares a term with the conclusion and shares a common or middle term not present in the conclusion.
	Premise	A premise is a previous statement or proposition from which another is inferred as a conclusion.
	Conclusion	A conclusion is a judgment or decision reached through reasoning.

Table 39 - Earth thinking Deductive reasoning component principles

EARTH THINKING – INDUCTIVE REASONING		
EARTH COMPONENT	**PRINCIPLE**	**DESCRIPTION**
INDUCTIVE REASONING	Generalization	A generalization is the expansion of a concept with less specific criteria. Generalizations are one of the foundational elements of logic and reasoning. Generalizations are essential to inferences.
	Hypothesis	A hypothesis is a supposition or explanation proposed based on limited evidence as a starting point for further investigation.
	Experiment	An experiment is a procedure with the aim of verifying, refuting, or establishing a hypothesis. An experiment can also be a detailed investigation or a test of the performance, qualities, or suitability of something.
	Scientific Method	The scientific method is a procedure that has characterized the study of the sciences since the 17th century. The method consists in systematic observation, measurement, and experiment, and the formulation, testing, and modification of hypotheses.
	Conclusion	A conclusion is a judgment or decision reached by reasoning.

Table 40 - Earth thinking Inductive reasoning component principles

EARTH THINKING – ABDUCTIVE REASONING		
EARTH COMPONENT	**PRINCIPLE**	**DESCRIPTION**
ABDUCTIVE REASONING	Causality	A relationship between two events, where the first event (the cause) induces the second event (the effect) to occur. It is a set of factors (cause) and their relationship to their phenomena (effect). The connection between a cause and an effect is also called a causal nexus.
	Occam's Razor	Named after William of Ockham (1287 – 1347), Occam's Razor is a principle of economy and succinctness in problem-solving stating that among competing hypotheses, the one with the fewest assumptions should be selected. More complicated solutions may prove correct, however, in the absence of evidence, the fewer assumptions that are employed the better.
	Decomposition	Decomposition during reasoning is the act of breaking down a problem into more manageable parts for easier analysis. Decomposition also assists in organizing concepts and promotes methodical analysis.
	Simplicity	Simplicity is expressed during reasoning with economy of thought, Occam's razor, minimal solutions, essential evidence, and identifying key pivots.
	How? & Why?	Two of the most useful questions in the thinker's toolkit. Ask "how?" and "why?" frequently to probe and deepen your analysis.
	Conclusion	A conclusion is a judgment or decision reached by reasoning.

Table 41 - Earth thinking Abductive reasoning component principles

Appendix-2 – Air Components & Principles Summary

AIR THINKING – INVESTIGATION		
AIR COMPONENT	**PRINCIPLE**	**DESCRIPTION**
INVESTI-GATION	Curiosity	Curiosity is the desire to know and learn about something. It is characteristic of inquisitive thinking, exploration, investigation and learning. It represents a thirst for knowledge and mental interest in a subject of inquiry.
	Examination	Examination is a detailed inspection or investigation. The objective is to scrutinize and inspect something. Inspection is the act of carefully examining or scrutinizing something. All your senses and powers of observation are employed.
	Experimentation	Experimentation is the act of conducting a test under controlled conditions to demonstrate a known truth, to examine the validity of a hypothesis, or to determine the efficacy of a process.
	Exploration	Exploration is an analysis of an idea, concept, proposal, subject or theme that is usually unfamiliar to learn more about it.
	Inquiry	Inquiry is the act of asking for information. It is a probe or query to seek information about a matter of interest.

Table 42 - Air thinking Investigation component principles

AIR THINKING – INCUBATION		
AIR COMPO-NENT	PRINCIPLE	DESCRIPTION
INCUBA-TION	Breaking Conditioning	Conditioning is a kind of learning where a mental association is made between behavior and the consequence of that behavior. Behaviors are reinforced or discouraged through rewards and punishments.
	Contemplation	Contemplation is deep reflective thought about a subject. Contemplation is used to incubate ideas through steady reflective thought on a matter.
	Eureka Effect	The Eureka effect is a sudden flash of insight into a problem. This creates a sudden understanding of a previously incomprehensible problem or concept.
	Problem Reformulation	Reformulating the problem statement gets you to question the basis of the analysis. Problem reformulation is the act of redefining the original problem from a different perspective, or approach.
	Unconventional Thinking	Thinking unconventionally incubates ideas because thinking about an issue in a different way that you normally do takes you down avenues that you would not normally explore which can be a source of innovation.

Table 43 - Air thinking Incubation component principles

AIR THINKING – INSIGHT		
AIR COMPONENT	**PRINCIPLE**	**DESCRIPTION**
INSIGHT	Flexibility	Mental agility is the ability of your mind to think in new and innovative ways.
	Intuition	Intuition is the ability to understand something without conscious thought or reasoning. Intuition can produce an insightful observation or an innovative idea. Intuition helps you take advantage of serendipity.
	Mental Fluency	Mental Fluency is the ease of cognition. It is a measure of how easily experiences, information, and decisions can be processed.
	Comparison (Similarity & Difference)	Looking for elements of commonality or areas of differences can germinate an idea. They can serve as starting points for thinking journeys and new paths to explore. Similarities and differences generate insight by giving you predictive qualities, common characteristics, and new mental models to work with.

Table 44 - Air thinking Insight component principles

AIR THINKING – INNOVATION		
AIR COMPONENT	**PRINCIPLE**	**DESCRIPTION**
INNOVATION	Brainstorm	Brainstorming is a specific technique for idea generation.
	Collaborative Creativity	Collaborative creativity is the act of working together with another person or with a group to stimulate innovation, imagination, and inventiveness.
	Gedanken	A Gedanken experiment is a thought exercise. It is a test of a concept or idea carried out mentally.
	Innovation factors	Methodical and deliberate idea generation can produce innovation. This is the intentional and conscious practice of generating ideas through the innovation factor idea seeds.
	Visualization	Visualization is mental imagery that is a representation of the physical world. Memory models play a vital role in memory and thinking. Visualization can be used to affect your thoughts, abilities, and expectations.

Table 45 - Air thinking Innovation component principles

Appendix-3 – Water Components & Principles Summary

WATER THINKING – LINKING		
WATER COMPONENT	PRINCIPLE	DESCRIPTION
LINKING	Association	An association is a connection or cooperative link between people, places, organizations, things, or concepts. Alliances, coalitions, puzzle pieces, interchangeable parts, affiliations, relationships, and bonds are examples.
	Cross-Fertilization	Used in the sense of cross-fertilization of ideas. Taking concepts from one field or discipline and applying them to a different one. The cross-fertilization creates a link between two fields of study. Inter-disciplinary studies (e.g. biomedical engineering) is an example of cross-fertilization.
	Decomposition	Breaking down a complex subject or concept into component elements or simpler constituents. Decomposition assists in comprehension of the interrelationship between elements in a system creating conceptual links between constituent elements. For example, the human body is composed of bone, flesh, blood, organs, and muscle as some of the constituent elements.
	Organization	A grouping, positioning, alignment or ordering of objects, concepts, people, or things with the purpose of identifying links between them.
	Patterns	A pattern is a recurrent design, or intelligible form of something. A model or design used as a template for other works. The blueprint for a home or a technical schematic for a manufactured component are examples of patterns.

Table 46 - Water thinking Linking component principles

WATER THINKING – PERSPECTIVE		
WATER COMPO-NENT	**PRINCIPLE**	**DESCRIPTION**
PERSPEC-TIVE	Big Picture & Maps	The big picture is a diagrammatic representation of a concept showing relevant major features. A map is a diagrammatic representation of a geographical area or a conceptual system. The principle of the big picture involves understanding the greater context of a problem or subject. The objective is to understand the greater environment upon which elements of your problem are nestled within.
	Ecology & System	The ecology is the relationship of things and their environment. The mental ecology is a system of concepts and their associated context. A system is a set of interdependent connected components forming an integrated complex whole.
	Framework	A basic structure underlying a system, concept or idea. A conceptual framework is the essential supporting skeleton, scaffolding, infrastructure, and chassis for a system. The framework provides a basis for understanding a whole system.
	Planning	Planning is the act of creating a procedure to achieve an objective. Planning is turning ideas into reality. It orchestrates resources, people, information, schedules, budgets, and decisions. Developing a plan is only possible by comprehending the big picture, and conceptual framework.
	Viewpoint	A viewpoint is a position from which something is observed, it is a certain attitude or way of considering a matter. Viewpoints can create reality filters and belief structures that change how we see the world.

Table 47 - Water thinking Perspective component principles

WATER THINKING – SYNTHESIS		
WATER COMPONENT	**PRINCIPLE**	**DESCRIPTION**
SYNTHESIS	Compare & Contrast	A comparison is a study of differences or similarities between two things. To contrast or juxtapose is to identify distinctive qualities and differences between two things.
	Conclusion & Summary	A summary is an account of the main points of a concept or idea. A conclusion is a judgment or decision reached by reasoning. Summaries and conclusions produce a synthesis through analysis and thinking.
	Permutation & Combination	A combination is a joining or merging of different parts where the component elements were individually distinct. A permutation is one of several possible variations, in which a set or number of things are ordered or arranged. The permutation is the act of changing the arrangement.
	Thesis & Antithesis	A thesis is a statement or theory that is put forward as a premise to be proved. An antithesis is a thing that is the direct opposite of the thesis. An analysis of a thesis and antithesis can generate a synthesis.
	Tradeoffs & Compromise	A trade-off is a balance achieved between two desirable but incompatible features. One quality may be favored based on the requirements and objectives of the system. A compromise is a settlement or agreement of a dispute that is reached by each side making concessions.

Table 48 - Water thinking Synthesis component principles

WATER THINKING – PIVOTS		
WATER COMPONENT	**PRINCIPLE**	**DESCRIPTION**
PIVOTS	Anchor	A conceptual anchor is a central idea, or thing which serves as a reference point or foundation concept. Concept anchors are the basis from which other ideas revolve.
	Bottlenecks	A bottleneck is a point of congestion or blockage. It is the point in a system or process where many other parts must pass through. For example, in a chemical reaction, it is rate-limiting factor. Bottlenecks are often where pivots occur.
	Catalyst	A catalyst is something that precipitates an event. It is a concept or idea which facilitates the completion or progress of a project. A catalyst facilitates the emergence of a pivot.
	Tipping Point	The tipping point is a point where dramatic change happens in a system. For example, when an idea is suddenly accepted by most people in a population. An idea goes viral by reaching a tipping point to "infect" the minds of many. The tipping point is a pivot.
	Trend	A trend is a general direction of observable outcomes from a system. A broad tendency of beliefs held by many people, or a consensus. A central focus of social attention for a time. After a pivotal event has occurred, a trend is created.

Table 49 - Water thinking Pivotrs component principles

Appendix-4 – Fire Components & Principles Summary

FIRE THINKING – DECISIONS		
FIRE COMPONENT	**PRINCIPLE**	**DESCRIPTION**
DECISIONS	Goals	The goal describes the ideal solution and objectives that a decision is trying to achieve. The goal encompasses the problem statement to be addressed with the decision.
	Constraints	Constraints describe the requirements and restrictions that your final choice or solution must conform to.
	Alternatives	Alternatives are the choices, possibilities and options that a decision will select from.
	Criteria	Criteria are factors that play a role in decision making. They are principles, measures, standards, or trade-offs that should be considered during the decision-making process.
	Consequences	The consequences describe the worst-case scenarios, contingencies, and repercussions that can result from a decision
	Selection	Selection is the process of picking between alternatives taking into consideration the goals, constraints, criteria and consequences.

Table 50 - Fire thinking Decisions component principles

FIRE THINKING – JUDGMENT		
FIRE COMPONENT	**PRINCIPLE**	**DESCRIPTION**
JUDGMENT	Experience	Experience encompasses your prowess, skill, knowledge and history in a subject. These are used to make good judgments.
	Fallacies of Thinking	The fallacies of thinking are mental traps which are good to avoid in the evaluation process.
	Objectivity	Bias is a partiality, favoritism, and prejudice towards one thing, person, or idea over another. Objectivity and impartiality free of bias are desirable when making judgments.
	Scrutiny	Scrutiny is the critical assessment and examination of an idea or proposal. You can assess the quality of a solution through its relevancy, efficacy, usefulness and benefits with respect to a problem. The objective of scrutiny is to carefully assess a thing, idea, situation, or proposal.
	Wisdom	Wisdom is the soundness of an action or decision with respect to the application of experience, knowledge, and good judgment. Wisdom is the body of knowledge and principles in a society which express sagacity, prudence, sophistication, and common sense.

Table 51 - Fire thinking Judgment component principles

Benjamin Cheung
180

FIRE THINKING – CONTINGENCY		
FIRE COMPONENT	**PRINCIPLE**	**DESCRIPTION**
CONTINGENCY	Vulnerability	A vulnerable point is a susceptibility or liability with respect to a threat or hazard.
	Hazard	A hazard is a danger or risk. Hazards represent uncertainties and complications that can give rise to a crisis.
	Response	A response is a predefined reaction to a hazard. Responses are alternatives and adaptations that are used to mitigate the effect of a crisis. Responses are designed to detect, manage, recover from, and anticipate hazards. Responses can improve and redefine proposed solutions to a problem.
	Contingency Plan	A contingency plan is a procedure or set of activities. With respect contingency planning, plans are a prearranged strategy to respond to a consequence or hazard. Plans need to account for the resources and capabilities of the system.

Table 52 - Fire thinking Contingency component principles

FIRE THINKING – VALIDITY		
FIRE COMPONENT	**PRINCIPLE**	**DESCRIPTION**
VALIDITY	Standards (Criterion of Truth)	In epistemology, the criteria of truth are standards that are used to judge the accuracy of statements and claims. They are tools of verification. These tests of truth are used to separate truth from falsehood. A standard is a measure by which evaluations can be compared against. It is widely accepted baseline norm.
	Consistency (Construct Validity)	Construct validity gauges if the measure is consistent with the theoretical concept being measured. Tests of validity are designed to support or refute the construct validity.
	Prediction	Prediction is being able to foretell a future event or trend. The forecast is inferred from evidence, knowledge, and experience. Valid information has cause and effect information that has predictive value.
	Reliability	Validity and reliability go hand in hand. Reliability is the dependability and trustworthiness of a measurement. It is the degree to which the measure is consistent. Repeated measurements are reliable if they yield similar results.

Table 53 - Fire thinking Validty component principles

Part IV – References

Appendix-9 - References

References

Aczel, A. D., & Sounderpandian, J. (2005). *Complete Business Statistics.* New Delhi: MacGraw Hill Publishing Company, Limited.

Amabile, T. M. (1996). *Creativity in Context.* Boulder, CO, USA: Westview Press.

Aristotle. (2012). *The Organon: The Works of Aristotle on Logic.* (R. B. Jones, Ed., E. M. Edghill, A. J. Jenkinson, G. R. Mure, & W. A. Pickard-Cambridge, Trans.) CreateSpace Independent Publishing Platform.

Aristotle. (2015). *On Sophistical Refutations (Sophistici Elenchi).* (P.-C. W. A., Trans.) South Australia: University of Adelaide.

Aristotle. (350 BCE). *Posterior Analytics.* (G. R. Mure, Trans.) Cambridge, Massachusetts, USA: MIT Classics. Retrieved from http://classics.mit.edu/Aristotle/posterior.html

Bacon, F., & Kitchin, G. (2000). *The Advancement of Learning* (1st Paul Dry Books Edition ed.). Philadelphia, PA, USA: Paul Dry Books.

Barabasi, A.-L. (2014). *Linked: How Everything is Connected to Everything Else and What It Means for Business, Science and Everyday Life.* New York City, NY, USA: Basic Books.

Barzun, J. (May 15, 2001). *From Dawn to Decadence: 1500 to the Present: 500 Years of Western Cultural Life* (1 ed.). New York, NY, USA: Harper Perennial.

Bennett, B. (2012). *Logically Fallacious: The Ultimate Collection of Over 300 Logical Fallacies* (Academic Edition ed.). Sudbury, Massachusetts, USA: eBookIt.com.

Cheung, B. (2003). *32 Innovation Factors.* Bloomington, Indiana, USA: Xlibris Corporation.

Cheung, B. (2003). *3G Cellular Systems in 90 Minutes.* Philadelphia, PA, USA: Xlibris Corporation.

Cheung, B. (2005). *Renewable Systems in 90 Minutes.* Philadelphia, PA, USA: Xlibris Corporation.

Cheung, B. (2005). *Robotics in 90 minutes.* Philadelphia, PA, USA: Xlibris Corporation.

Cheung, B., Gopal, K., DaSilva, V., Dwyer, T., Sudarsan, P., & Parasher, B. (2014). *USA Patent No. 8,755,805 B2.*

Cheung, B., Khawer, M. R., Sudarsan, P., & Gayde, R. S. (2018, March 13). *United States of America Patent No. 9,918,232.*

Cheung, B., N., K., N., K. G., & Putman, A. E. (2008). *USA Patent No. 7,443,804 B2.*

Childs, D. R., & Dietrich, S. (2002). *Contingency Planning and Disaster Recovery: A Small Business Guide* (1st ed.). Hoboken, New Jersey, USA: Wiley Publishing.

Copi, I. M., Cohen, C., & Flage, D. E. (2007). *Essentials of Logic* (Second ed.). Upper Saddle River, New Jersey, USA: Pearson Education.

D'Antonio, M. (2008). *A Ball, a Dog, and a Monkey: 1957 -- The Space Race Begins* (Reprint ed.). Simon & Schuster.

Duncker, K. (1945). On Problem Solving . *Psychological Monographs, 58*(5). doi:DOI: 10.1037/h0093599

Encyclopedia Britannica (15th ed., Vol. III: Micropedia). (Founded 1768).

Fadem, T. J. (2008). *The Art of Asking: Ask Better Questions, Get Better Answers* (1st ed.). Upper Saddle River, New Jersey, USA: Financial Times (FT) Press.

Fermi, L. (1961). *The Story of Atomic Energy (World Landmark books, 48).* New York City, New York, USA: Random House.

Franklin, J. (2002). *The Science of Conjecture: Evidence and Probability before Pascal* (Annotated Edition ed.). Baltimore, Maryland, USA: Johns Hopkins University Press.

Gelb, M. J. (2000). *How to Think Like Leonardo da Vinci: Seven Steps to Genius Every Day* (Reissue ed.). New York, NY, USA: Dell Publishing.

Gharajedgaghi, J. (2005). *Systems Thinking: Managing Chaos and Complexity : a Platform for Designing Business Architecture* (2nd ed.). Waltham, Massachusetts, USA: Butterworth-Heinemann.

Gladwell, M. (2002). *The Tipping Point: How Little Things Can Make a Big Difference.* New York City, NY, USA: Back Bay Books.

Guilford, J. P. (1967). *The Nature of Human Intelligence.* New York, NY, USA: McGraw-Hill.

Hawkings, J., & Blakeslee, S. (2005). *On Intelligence: How a New Understanding of the Brain Will Lead to the Creation of Truly Intelligent Machines* (Reprint ed.). New York City, NY, USA: St. Martin's Griffin.

Herbert, F. (1990). *Dune.* New York City, NY, USA: Ace Books.

Hoenig, C. (2000). *The Problem-Solving Journey, Your Guide for Making Decisions and Getting Results.* New York City: Perseus Publishing.

Hogarth, R. M. (1991). *Judgment and Choice: The Psychology of Decision* (Second ed.). Chichester, UK: Wiley.

Hurley, P. J. (2011). *A Concise Introduction to Logic* (11th ed.). Belmont, CA, USA: Wadsworth Publishing.

Koestler, A. (1964). *The Act of Creation.* New York City, NY, USA: Dell publishing company.

Langley, P., & Jones, R. (1988). A Computational Model of Scientific Insights. (R. Sternberg, Ed.) *The Nature of Creativity. Contemporary Psychological Perspectives*, 177-201.

Lehrer, J. (2010). *How We Decide* (Reprint ed.). New York City, New York, USA: Mariner Books.

Lieberman, D. J. (2006). *How to Change Anybody, Proven Techniques to Reshape Anyone's Attitude, Behavior, Feelings, or Beliefs.* New York, NY, USA: St. Martin's Griffin.

Maney, K. (2010). *Trade-Off: Why Some Things Catch On, and Others Don't* (1st ed.). New York City, NY, USA: Crown Business.

McInerny, D. Q. (2005). *Being Logical: A Guide to Good Thinking* (Reprint ed.). New York City, NY, USA: Random House Trade Paperbacks.

McKaughan, D. J. (2008). From Ugly Duckling to Swan: C. S. Peirce, Abduction, and the Pursuit of Scientific Theories. *Transactions of the Charles S. Peirce Society, 44*(3 (Summer)), pp. 446-468.

Mednick, S. (1962). The Associative Basis of the Creative Process. (K. J. Holyoak, Ed.) *Psychological Review, 69*(3), 220-232. doi:DOI: 10.1037/h0048850

Molles, M. (2012). *Ecology: Concepts and Applications* (7th International ed.). New York City, New York, USA: McGraw-Hill Education.

Nijstad, B. A., & Stroebe, W. (2006). How the Group Affects the Mind: A Cognitive Model of Idea Generation in Groups. *Personality and Social Psychology Review, 10*(3), 186-213. doi:DOI: 10.1207/s15327957pspr1003_1

Offner, A. K., Kramer, T. J., & Winter, J. P. (1996). The Effects of Facilitation, Recording, and Pauses on Group Brainstorming. *Small Group Research, 27*(2), 283-298. doi:DOI: 10.1177/1046496496272005

Osborn, A. F. (1953). *Applied Imagination, Principles and Procedures of Creative Problem-Solving.* New York City, NY, USA: Scribner.

Pasteur, L. (1854, December 7). Lecture at University of Lille.

Paulus, P. B., & Yang, H. C. (2000). Idea generation in groups: A basis for creativity in organizations. *Organizational Behavior and Human Decision Processes, 82*(1), 76-87. doi:DOI: 10.1006/obhd.2000.2888

Peirce, C. S. (1992). *The Essential Peirce: Selected Philosophical Writings* (Vol. 2). Bloomington, Indiana, USA: Indiana University Press.

Plato. (360 BC). *Timeus.* Athens, Greece: MIT Classics. Retrieved from http://classics.mit.edu/Plato/timaeus.1b.txt

Poincare, H. (1929). *The Foundations of Science: Science and Hypothesis, The Value of Science, Science and Method* (Reissue edition (Dec 11, 2014) ed.). (G. B. Halsted, Trans.) Cambridge City, Cambridge, UK: Cambridge University Press.

Pugh, S. (1981, March). Concept Selection: a Method that Works. *Review of design methodology. Proceedings international conference on engineering design*, 497-506.

Rathmanner, S., & Hutter, M. (2011, June 3). A philosophical Treatise of Universal Induction. *Entropy, 13*(6), 1076-1136.

Sahakian, W. S., & Sahakian, M. L. (1993). *Ideas of the Great Philosophers.* New York City, New York, USA: Barnes & Noble Publishing.

Segal, E. (2004). Incubation in Insight Problem Solving. *Creativity Research Journal, 16*(1), 141-148.

Simon, H. A. (1966). Scientific Discovery and the Psychology of Problem Solving. (R. Colodny, Ed.) *Mind and Cosmos*, 22-40. doi:DOI: 10.1007/978-94-010-9521-1_16

Simplicius. (2011). *On Aristotle Physics 1.3-4 (Ancient Commentators on Aristotle).* (C. Taylor, & P. Huby, Trans.) London, England: Bristol Classical Press.

Sober, E. (2015). *Ockham's Razors: A User's Manual.* Cambridge, England, UK: Cambridge University Press.

Terrell, D. B. (1967). *Logic, a Modern Introduction to Deductive Reasoning.* New York City, New York, USA: Holt, Rinehart and Winston.

Thompson, L. (2003). Improving the Creativity of Organizational Work Groups. *Academy of Management Executive, 17*(1), 96-109. doi:DOI: 10.5465/AME.2003.9474814

Thompson, L., Loewenstein, J., & Gentner, D. (2000). Avoiding Missed Opportunities in Managerial Life: Analogical Training More Powerful than Individual Case Training. *Organizational Behavior and Human Decision Processes, 82*(1), 60-75. doi:DOI: 10.1006/obhd.2000.2887

Tro, N. J. (2016). *Chemistry: A Molecular Approach* (4th ed.). New York City, New York, USA: Pearson.

Trochim, W. M. (2001). *The Research Methods Knowledge Base* (Second ed.). Cincinnati, OH, USA: Atomic Dog Publishing. Retrieved from http://www.atomicdogpublishing.com

Urry, L. A., Cain, M. L., Wasserman, S. A., & Minorsky, P. V. (2016). *Biology* (11th ed.). New York City, New York, USA: Pearson.

Van de Ven, A. H., & Delbecq, A. L. (1974). The Effectiveness of Nominal, Delphi, and Interacting Group Decision Making Processes. *Academy of Management Journal, 17*(4), 605-621.

Van Gundy, A. B. (1988). *Techniques of Structured Problem Solving* (Second ed.). New York City: Van Nostrand Reinhold.

Vera, D., & Crossan, M. (2005). Improvisation and Innovative Performance in Teams. *Organization Science, 16*(3), 203-224.

Vidal, R., Mulet, E., & Gomez-Senent, E. (2004). Effectiveness of the Means of Expression in Creative Problem-Solving in Design Groups. *Journal of Engineering Design, 15*(3), 285-298. doi:DOI: 10.1080/09544820410001697587

Voltaire. (1808). Maxims and reflections on different topics of morality and politics. Paris.

Wallas, G. (1926). *The Art of Thought.* London, UK: Jonathan Cape.

Watson, J. D., & Crick, F. H. (1953). Molecular Structure of Nucleic Acids: A Structure for Deoxyribose Nucleic Acid. *Nature, 171*(4356), 737-738.

Webster's New World Dictionary (College ed.). (1984). Simon and Schuster.

Wells, F. L. (1911). Practice Effects in Free Association. *The American Journal of Psychology, 22*(1), 1-13. doi:DOI: 10.2307/1413074

Winston, W. (1994). *Operations Research: Applications and Algorithms* (3rd ed.). Belmont, California, USA: Duxbury Press.

Woodworth, R. S., & Schlosberg, H. (1960). *Experimental Psychology.* New York City, NY, USA: Henry Holt and Company.

Wozniak, S., & Smith, G. (2007). *iWoz: Computer Geek to Cult Icon: How I Invented the Personal Computer, Co-Founded Apple, and Had Fun Doing It* (Reprint ed.). New York City, NY, USA: W. W. Norton & Company.

Yaniv, I., & Meyer, D. E. (1987). Activation and Metacognition of Inaccessible Stored Information: Potential Bases of Incubation Effects in Problem Solving. *Journal of Experimental Psychology: Learning, Memory, and Cognition, 13*, 187-205.

Yeates, L. B. (2004). Thought Experimentation: A Cognitive Approach. Kensington, New South Wales, Australia: University of New South Wales.

Zannos, S. (2004). *The Life and Times of Archimedes (Biography From Ancient Civilizations Series).* Newark, Deleware, USA: Mitchell Lane Publishers, Inc.